Worship the Lord

With Gladness:
God's Children in Worship

Rita B. Hays

Abingdon Press
Nashville

ISBN: 9781426753305

PACP01110700-01

Editor: Daphna Flegal
Production Editor: Norma Bates
Designer: Kellie Green
Cover Designer: Keely Moore
Illustrations: Megan Jeffrey and Shutterstock

13 14 15 16 17 18 19 20 21 22—10 9 8 7 6 5 4 3 2 1

Printed in the USA

Contents

Worship the Lord With Gladness: God's Children in Worship

The curriculum piece *Worship the Lord With Gladness: God's Children in Worship* is designed to teach young elementary children (kindergarten – 3rd grade) about worship. Each lesson is based upon a Scripture verse that the children examine in detail. Activities, games, drama, role-play, reproducibles, and music are incorporated into the lessons. There is also an opportunity during each session for children to engage in worship. Take-home ideas for worship in the family and ways to reinforce the lessons in the home are provided.

Each lesson contains the following:

Worship Wisdom

Background material for the teacher.

Enter With Gladness

Gathering activities for children as they arrive for the worship study.

Bible Praise Notes

Children will examine the Scripture for the day.

Let's Learn to Worship

Activities, games, drama, role-play, reproducibles, and music help the children learn about the particular worship theme.

We Worship God

A time to put into practice what the children have learned.

My Family Helps Me Worship

Take-home ideas for worship in the home and reinforcing the lesson.

 # Come, Let's Worship God!

Bible Verse: I rejoiced with those who said to me,
"Let's go to the LORD's house!" (*Psalm 122:1*)

Children will:

- Examine the Bible verse.
- Explore the question: What is Worship?
- Learn about worship in both the Old and the New Testaments.
- Think about different styles of worship and various places to worship.

 # Worship Wisdom

The word *worship* means to "bow down to," "show reverence to," "pay homage to," or "honor God." When we worship, we offer thanksgiving, love, adoration, and praise to God. Worship reminds us that our journey of faith entails our continued devotion and loyalty to God as an expression of our trust in a God who covenants with us. Worship allows us a time, in our busy schedules, to center our thoughts on God and God's great love for us in Jesus Christ. True worship focuses on God, rather than the individual and his or her own needs and desires. Worship motivates us to humbly care for and serve others. We use our hearts, minds, and bodies when we worship.

The Bible provides a diverse picture of the ways people worshiped God, and Scripture mentions various worship settings. Examples from both the Old Testament and the New Testament show the importance of worship for the people of God. The children of Israel often stopped on their wilderness journey to erect altars to God and engage in worship. God instructed Moses to erect a tabernacle, a portable place of worship, which accompanied the Israelites on their wanderings in the wilderness and their conquest of the Promised Land. It contained the ark of the covenant or sacred chest, a container for the Ten Commandments that was eventually placed in the Temple in Jerusalem. Once they settled in the Promised Land, the Jewish people worshiped in the Temple built by Solomon. When the Jewish people dispersed, synagogues were built in villages and towns. Jesus worshiped in the synagogue in his hometown of Nazareth, and he also made trips to Jerusalem to worship in the Temple. The first Christians worshiped in homes, until eventually church buildings were erected.

Following in the footsteps of our biblical ancestors, we worship God today in a variety of ways and settings. What is important is our attitude in worship. The psalmist expresses for us the right mindset when worshiping God. The writer declared his gladness when entering the place of worship. While the words are attributed to David, we are not sure who wrote the words. Regardless, they are important words for us today as we approach God in worship. We should come before God with gladness in our hearts. We should respect and offer thanksgiving for our places of worship today. These are lessons we seek to teach our children about worship.

 **Enter With Gladness**

As the Children Arrive

Supplies: *praise CD, CD player*

- Play praise music as children arrive.

- Greet each child by name.

Decorate a Worship Bag

Supplies: Reproducibles 24-25—pp. 119-120, *scissors, paint pens or fabric crayons, cloth bags (available at craft stores)*

Preparation:

- *Photocopy the symbols (Reproducibles 24-25).*

- Give each child a cloth bag.

- Show the children the worship symbols. Let the children draw symbols on their bags.

- They may want to use the symbols as patterns. Let the children cut out the patterns and trace them onto their bags.

- Encourage the children to bring their worship bags with them to church. They might use their worship bags to carry their Bible and offering money.

Visit the Worship Center

Supplies: *table, cloth, items used in your worship service*

Preparation:

- *Set up a worship center at a visible location in your room. Cover a small table with a cloth.*

- *Place some items used in your worship service on the table. Items might include a cross, Bible, hymnal, candles, bulletin, and communion-ware.*

- Show the children the items on your worship center.

Ask: How is each item used in worship? Where do we find this item in the sanctuary?

 Bible Praise Notes

Learn the Bible Verse

Supplies: *Bibles*

- Show the children how to find Psalm 122:1 in the Bible. Read the verse to the children.

Say: The Psalms is a book of the Bible that offers praise to God. When we worship, we praise God. We speak, sing, or listen to words that remind us of how good and powerful God is. We learn that God loves us and that Jesus is our friend.

- Divide the children into two groups. Have one group say, "*I rejoiced with those who said to me.*" Have the other group say, "*Let's go to the LORD's house!*"

- Repeat this several times, and then reverse what each group says.

Happy Face Puppet

Supplies: *small paper plates, markers or crayons, craft sticks, masking tape*

- Give each child a paper plate. Have the children draw happy faces on the plates.

- Give each child a craft stick and a piece of tape. Have the children tape the craft sticks to the backs of the plates.

Ask: What makes you glad (happy) when you come to worship at church?

- When a child names something, have all the children wave their puppets, and say the Bible verse, "I rejoiced with those who said to me, 'Let's go to the LORD's house!'" (Psalm 122:1).

- Let the children wave their puppets as they sing "Happy, Happy Children Now" to the tune of "Twinkle, Twinkle Little Star."

Say: The word *worship* means to *bow down to God.* When you sing the word *bow* move your puppets in a motion of bowing down to God.

- Show the children how to do this motion. Remind the children that to bow down to God is a way to show God honor and great love.

Happy, Happy Children Now
(Tune: "Twinkle, Twinkle, Little Star")

Happy, happy children now
Come to worship God and bow.
Offer praise in many ways,
Thanks to God for each new day.
Happy, happy children now
Come to worship God and bow.

 # Let's Learn to Worship

Bible People Worshiped God

Supplies: *Bible,* Reproducible 1—p. 96

Preparation:

- *Photocopy "Bible People Worshiped God" (Reproducible 1) for each child.*

- Give each child a copy. Encourage the children to find the drawing of the **altar**.

Say: The people worshiped God as they traveled in the wilderness with their leader Moses. They would stop in their travels to build altars to God as ways to honor God. These altars were often made of large stones.

- Encourage the children to find the drawing of the **tablets**.

Say: Moses received the Ten Commandments from God, written on tablets of stone.

- Read the words of the Ten Commandments to the children from the Bible (Exodus 20:1-17), or remind them of some of the commandments.

- Discuss the importance of the Ten Commandments for the people in Bible times and their importance for us today.

- Encourage the children to find the picture of the **tabernacle**.

Say: The tabernacle was a large tent of worship that the people could carry with them as they traveled. They set up the tabernacle each

time they stopped. They took the tabernacle down each time they were ready to move to a new place.

- Encourage the children to find the drawing of the **Temple**.

Say: The Temple was a special place to worship God and took several years to build. It had many rooms and was beautifully decorated.

- Encourage the children to find the drawing of the **scroll**.

Say: Bible people read from a scroll to learn about God. Today we read from the Bible.

- Remind the children that just as Bible people worshiped God in many places, they can also worship God in many places. They can worship God at camp, in their homes, or in nature. However, the church is a special and important place to worship God.

Worship Charades

Say: There are many ways to worship God. No one way is the right way or the best way.

- Play a game of worship charades. Whisper to one child a way of worshiping God. Let that child act out that way of worshiping for the other children.

- When a child guesses the way of worship, that child becomes the one to act out next.

- Here are some of the charade actions you might whisper: praying, reading the Bible, singing, lifting hands in praise, kneeling, bowing, playing an instrument, dancing.

Worship Motion

Supplies: *praise CD, CD player, scarves or pieces of fabric*

- Play a CD of praise music. Encourage the children to imitate what you do: lift your hands in praise of God; bow down to God; clap your hands to thank God.

- Let the children dance to the music. Give the children scarves or pieces of fabric. Let them wave their scarves or pieces of fabric as the music plays.

Different Styles of Worship

Supplies: Reproducible 2—p. 97, *crayons or pencils*

Preparation:

- *Photocopy "Worship Today" (Reproducible 2) for each child.*

Say: There are many different churches. Each church has a different way of worshiping God. Some churches have a choir that sings, while other churches use a band to play music. In some churches there is a piano and/or an organ, and in others churches the musician plays a guitar. In some churches the ministers wear a robe and in other churches the minister may wear a suit, casual clothes, or jeans. In some churches, the worshipers sit in pews, while in other churches they may sit in chairs. Some churches meet in a church building in a room called a sanctuary, while other churches meet in a school or office building.

Ask: What about your church? Does your church have a choir? Does your minister wear a robe? Does your church use acolytes in the service? Do the worshipers in your church sit in pews or chairs?

Say: Many people and many churches seek to worship God, but may do so in different ways. God honors all of the ways we worship.

- Give each child a copy of "Worship Today." Have the children circle the pictures of items they find in their own church.

- Talk about the other items that might be used in worship by other churches.

Worship Around the World

Supplies: *pictures of people in other countries worshiping God (downloadable from AbingdonPress.com/downloads)*

Preparation:

- *Download and print the pictures that show people in other countries worshiping God.*

- Show the children the pictures. Let the children talk about the various ways and places they see people worshiping God.

- Remind the children that people worship God in many languages. Teach the children the Spanish name for God—*Dios.* Other names for God may be found online. Invite a person who speaks Spanish to say the Lord's Prayer for the children in the Spanish language.

- Let the children work together to place the pictures in the shape of a cross on the floor.

- Gather the children in a circle around the cross, and offer a prayer for people around the world. Give thanks that people all around the world worship God in many ways and places, and by using many languages.

We Worship God

Supplies: *shofar*

- Call your children to the worship time using a shofar—a horn blown to call the Jewish people to worship in the synagogue. (Inexpensive shofars can be ordered online, or you might borrow one from a Jewish friend.)

Synagogue Worship

Supplies: Leaders' Guide—p. 10, *praise CD, CD player, benches, mats, or rugs, dowel rod, butcher paper, Star of David, oil lamps, menorah, picture of Jewish synagogue, kippah (skull cap) or picture of a kippah, black ministerial robe, shawls or scarves, musical instruments*

Preparation:

- *Photocopy "My Family Helps Me Worship" (p. 10) for each child.*

- *Set up an area like a Jewish synagogue. Use benches, mats, or a rug for the children to sit on.*

- *Make some scrolls using a dowel rod and butcher paper. Write Psalm 122:1 on the scroll.*

- *Place a Star of David in the synagogue. Resources for making a Star of David can be found online.*

- *Place some oil lamps around the area. Display a menorah (candelabrum with seven candle holders).*

- *Look online for pictures of a Jewish synagogue and a kippah (skull cap). Print the pictures.*

- *Recruit a volunteer to play the role of the rabbi. Dress him in a black ministerial robe. Cover his head with a scarf or shawl.*

- *Provide head coverings for the children to wear.*

- *Let the children gather in the synagogue.*

Say: Men showed reverence for God by wearing kippahs (skull caps) on their heads. Jewish people covered their heads when they entered the synagogue for worship to show respect for God.

- Give each child a shawl or head covering. Show the children the picture of the kippah.

Say: Jesus was Jewish. He worshiped God in the synagogue. Sometimes he went to the Temple in Jerusalem to worship God. Today, Jewish people still worship God in synagogues. Early Christians worshiped God in synagogues. Later, they worshiped God in homes, until finally church buildings were constructed. Today, we remember the way Jesus worshiped God in the synagogue.

Synagogue Ideas

1. Have the rabbi unroll the scroll and read Psalm 122:1 to the children.

2. Reinforce the Bible verse learned in the Praise Notes section. Divide the children into two groups. Have one group say, *"I rejoiced with those who said to me."* Have the other group say, *"Let's go to the LORD's house!"*

3. Sing some praise songs. Select some of the children's favorite songs to sing.

4. Pass out musical instruments and let the children sing, "God is So Good"

God Is so Good.

God is so good.	God is my friend,
God is so good.	God is my friend,
God is so good.	God is my friend.
God's so good to me.	God's so good to me.

5. Teach the children the word *shalom.* Explain to the children that the Hebrew word means "God's peace." Have the children walk around and say the word to one another.

6. Invite an individual who is Jewish to share with the children about worship in the synagogue.

- *Send home "My Family Helps Me Worship" (p. 10) with each child.*

Pray: Thank you, God, for this time to learn about worship. We are happy to worship you in our church, in our homes, and in your world. Thank you for the gift of worship. Amen.

 # My Family Helps Me Worship

Come, Let's Worship God!

Your child learned that worship is praising and honoring God with our hearts, our minds, and our bodies. There are a variety of ways to worship.

Talk Points for the Week

Ask: What do you think the word *worship* means?

Ask: What is your favorite part of worship?

Family Worship

Set up a worship center in your home. Let the children in the family help you select a place for your worship center and items to place on the table.

How to Set Up Your Worship Center

1. Select a small table or card table.

2. Cover the worship center with a cloth. You might wish to select a cloth that is the color of the liturgical season in the church.

3. Place some symbols of worship on your worship table or altar. (Bible, cross, flowers, butterflies, candles)

Worship God With Scripture

Read Psalm 122:1: *I rejoiced with those who said to me, "Let's go to the Lord's house."*

Have family members say the verse together.

Share Gladness

Have family members share about what happens in worship that makes them glad.

Worship God With Songs

Sing together the following song.

Praise God, Praise God, All Ye Little Children

Praise God, praise God, all ye little children,
God is love, God is love,
Praise God, praise God, all ye little children
God is love, God is love.

Repeat, substituting the words, Thank God, Serve God, and Love God for Praise God.

Worship Litany

One: People worship God in many ways.

All: Our family worships God!

One: People worship God in many places.

All: Our family worships God!

One: People worship God speaking many languages.

All: Our family worships God!

One: People worship God using their hands, their feet, their voices, and their whole bodies.

All: Our family worships God!

One: People worship God at different times.

All: Our family worships God!

One: People worship God in nature, at camp, on vacation, in the home, and in the church.

All: Our family worships God!

One: Worship is the way we praise God, thank God, and honor God.

All: Our family worships God!

Prayer:

One: Thank you, God, for the gift of worship. Thank you, God, for this time to worship together as a family.

All: Amen.

Worship the Lord With Gladness: God's Children in Worship

2 Come to the Water - Baptism

Bible Verses: When Jesus was baptized, he immediately came up out of the water. Heaven was opened to him, and he saw the Spirit of God coming down like a dove and resting on him. A voice from heaven said, "This is my Son whom I dearly love; I find happiness in him." (*Matthew 3:16-17*)

Children will:
• Examine the Bible passage about Jesus' baptism.

• Explore the meaning of baptism.

• Learn the three modes of baptism in The United Methodist Church.

• Think about ways Jesus pleased God and ways children can please God.

Worship Wisdom

At our baptism, God claims each of us as beloved children of God. God reaches out with grace and offers us the gift of God's abiding presence and unmerited love. In our Wesleyan tradition, we describe this powerful and decisive action of God as *prevenient grace*. God continually reaches out to us throughout our entire lives, seeking to draw us closer to our Creator. God is forever wooing us, even when we stray away from God or deny God with our thoughts and actions. In our baptism, the church affirms God's everlasting love for us.

Furthermore, baptism expresses our belief that God calls us by name and begins God's redeeming work of salvation in each of our lives. While the primary agent in our baptism is God, the church plays a vital role. At our baptism, members of the body of Christ promise to nurture us in the faith and set an example for us of Christlike living.

We baptize infants in the Wesleyan tradition because we believe that God's grace and love are extended to us from the moment of our birth. Believing parents bring their infants to be baptized in the midst of a caring congregation that vows to partner with parents in raising their child in the Christian faith.

We do not believe that the amount of water matters. What matters most is that God is present and active in our baptism and in our lives. In The United Methodist Church, we baptize persons of all ages. Our three modes of baptism are immersion, sprinkling, and pouring, as we view all three forms of baptism as scriptural. United Methodists do not re-baptize because we believe God acted powerfully in each of our baptisms, whether we can remember the event or not.

John the Baptist baptized Jesus in the Jordan River. John, the son of the priest Zechariah and his wife Elizabeth, was a cousin of Jesus. John the Baptist was called by God to prepare the way for the coming of the Messiah. John the Baptist baptized individuals as a sign of their repentance. Jesus came to John to be baptized, not as a sign of repentance, however, but as a mark that his ministry had begun.

The dove is the symbol for the Holy Spirit. The Holy Spirit was present at Jesus' baptism, indicating to the observers that God was at work in Jesus' life and ministry. The Holy Spirit shows up at each baptism. No matter where our baptisms take place or what method is used, God is happy when we are baptized and begin our faith journey. Just as God dearly loved Jesus, God dearly loves us.

 **Enter With Gladness**

As the Children Arrive

Supplies: *CD with water sounds, CD player*

- Greet each child by name. Play water sounds.

Who Is Being Baptized?

Supplies: *Reproducible 3—p. 98, smiley face stickers, pencils*

Preparation:

- Photocopy *"Jesus Is Baptized"* (Reproducible 3) for each child.

- Give each child *"Jesus Is Baptized."* Let each child connect the dots. Help the children identify Jesus and the dove.

- Give each child a smiley face sticker.

Say: God was very happy when Jesus was baptized. God was pleased with Jesus.

Dove and Water

Supplies: *clothespins and coffee filters, one for each child; markers*

Say: Baptism is a special time in our church. Each time a person is baptized, we remember how much God loves us. Each person is special to God. God knows our names. A dove reminds us of baptism and of the Holy Spirit.

- Give each child a clothespin and a coffee filter. Show the children how to pinch their coffee filter in the middle and attach the clothespin. The clothespin makes the body of the dove and the coffee filter makes the wings.

- Have the children draw eyes on the dove, one on each side at the bottom of the clothespin, where it opens.

Visit the Worship Center

Supplies: *small table, white cloth, Bible, white candles, a shell, a dove, a basin and pitcher, water*

Preparation:

- *Set up a worship center on a small table in your room. Cover the table with a white cloth (the liturgical color for baptism).*

- *Place on the table a Bible, white candles, a shell (symbol of baptism), a dove (symbol of the Holy Spirit), and a basin and pitcher, filled with water.*

- Show the children some of the items at your worship center.

Say: You will hear a story about Jesus' baptism. Listen for the part of the story that mentions the dove. The dove represents the Holy Spirit. God sent the Holy Spirit as a sign that God was present with Jesus at his baptism.

- Pour water out of the pitcher into the basin. Let each child come forward and dip his or her dove into the water.

 Bible Praise Notes

Learn the Bible Story

Supplies: *small shells, one for each child*

Say: The symbol for baptism in the church is a shell. Sometimes when people were baptized in the early church, the minister dipped a shell in the water, scooped up water in the shell, and poured the water on the head of the person being baptized.

- Give each child a shell.

- Read *"Jesus is Baptized"* to the children.

Worship the Lord With Gladness: God's Children in Worship

- When the children hear the word **Jesus,** have them touch their hearts with their shells.

- When they hear the words **John the Baptist**, have them touch their foreheads with the shells.

- When the children hear the word **baptized**, have them pretend they are scooping up water with their shells and pouring it out of their shells.

- Demonstrate the motions for the children and let them practice.

Jesus Is Baptized

John the Baptist (touch forehead with shell) was sent by God to tell people about **Jesus** (touch heart with shell). He **baptized** (scoop and pour from shell) many people in the Jordan River.

One day, **John the Baptist** (touch forehead with shell) saw **Jesus** (touch heart with shell) coming toward him. **John the Baptist** (touch forehead with shell) was very surprised when **Jesus** (touch heart with shell) told him that he wanted to be **baptized** (scoop and pour from shell).

John the Baptist (touch forehead with shell) believed that he was unworthy to **baptize** (scoop and pour from shell) **Jesus** (touch heart with shell).

However, **Jesus** (touch heart with shell) wanted to be **baptized** (scoop and pour from shell).

John the Baptist (touch forehead with shell) did as **Jesus** (touch heart with shell) asked and **baptized** (scoop and pour from shell) him in the river.

When **Jesus** (touch heart with shell) came out of the water, a dove landed on him. God sent the Holy Spirit to be with **Jesus** (touch heart with shell) as he was **baptized** (scoop and pour from shell).

God said to **Jesus** (touch heart with shell), "This is my Son whom I dearly love; I find happiness in him."

Shell and Shark Game

Supplies: Reproducible 4—p. 99, scissors, bag

Preparation:

- Photocopy several copies of "Shell and Shark Game" (Reproducible 4).

- Cut out the pictures of the shell and shark and place in a bag.

- Divide the children into two teams. Rotate turns from team to team as each child reaches into the bag and draws out either a picture of a shell or a picture of a shark.

- If a child draws a picture of a shark, his or her team loses a turn.

- If a child draws a picture of a shell, that child answers a question about the Bible lesson. If he or she answers correctly, that child's team keeps the picture of the shell. If the child answers the question incorrectly, the picture of the shell is returned to the bag and the other team gets to draw from the bag.

- The team who collects the most shell pictures wins the game.

Here are some questions you might ask:

Who baptized Jesus? (John the Baptist)

What river was Jesus baptized in? (Jordan)

What landed on Jesus when he came out of the water? (dove)

What is the dove a symbol for? (Holy Spirit)

What is the shell a symbol for? (baptism)

Who did God send to tell people about Jesus? (John the Baptist)

True or False: Jesus wanted John the Baptist to baptize him. (true)

True or False: God was pleased with Jesus. (true)

True or False: Jesus was the only person John baptized. (false)

True or False: At his baptism God sent the Holy Spirit to be with Jesus. (true)

True or False: God was happy when Jesus was baptized. (true)

 Let's Learn to Worship

Baptismal Tour

Supplies: *pitcher, basin, small plastic swimming pool, water, pictures of persons being baptized (downloadable from AbingdonPress.com/downloads), laminate*

Preparation:

- *Place a pitcher and basin at a location in your church, outside your classroom if possible.*

- *Purchase or borrow a small plastic swimming pool and fill with water. If weather permits, place your swimming pool outside.*

- *Download and print the pictures of persons being baptized.*

- *Laminate the pictures and place them face down in the pool.*

Say: People are usually baptized in a church building.

- Take the children to the sanctuary to see the baptismal font.

Say: Sprinkling is one of the ways we baptize in our church. The minister takes some water in his or her hand and sprinkles it over the head of the person being baptized.

- Let the children look in the baptismal font.

Ask: When have you seen sprinkling used in a baptism?

- Have the children say the word *sprinkling* over and over as they march to their next location.

- Take the children to the location where you have the pitcher and basin.

Say: Pouring is another way we baptize in our church. The minister asks the person being baptized to kneel. The pastor pours water on the head of the person kneeling.

- Have the children say the word *pouring* several times.

Ask: Have your ever seen pouring used in a baptism?

- Have the children say the words *sprinkling* and *pouring* several times as they march to their next location.

- Take the children to the pool. *Be sure and have additional volunteers present at the pool, and never leave any child unattended.*

Say: Some people are baptized in a pool, located in the church. We call this a baptismal pool. The person being baptized walks into the pool with the minister and is dipped into the water. Some churches do not have a baptismal pool. If not, the person might be baptized at another church where there is a baptismal pool. However, some people might be baptized in a creek. We call this way of being baptized *immersion.*

Ask: Have you ever seen someone baptized by immersion?

Note: *Some churches have baptismal pools. If your church has a baptismal pool in your sanctuary, take your children to that location to share about immersion, and then take them to the pool location.*

- Let the children watch as you take each picture depicting baptism out of the pool and show it to the children. Let the water drip from the picture. As you show the children each picture ask them:

> Where is the person being baptized? *(church, creek, camp, outside)*
>
> Who is being baptized?
>
> Who is baptizing the person? *(pastor)*
>
> Who is watching the baptism?
>
> Is the person being baptized by sprinkling, by pouring, or by immersion?
>
> What is put on the head or body of the person being baptized? *(water)*

- Have the children march back to the classroom saying the words *sprinkling, pouring, immersion.*

- Encourage the children to watch carefully the next time a baptism takes place in worship.

Say: Baptism is a happy time for the church and for the family of the person being baptized. Baptism is also a happy time for God.

The Symbol of Baptism

Supplies: *baby food jars with lids, one for each child; small shells; stickers (shell, dove, smiley face)*

- Give each child a baby food jar. Let the children decorate the outside of their jars with stickers that symbolize baptism.

Say: When Jesus was baptized God was very happy. Jesus lived his life in a way that pleased God and made God very happy. Like Jesus, we want to do things that please God. We want to live our lives in such a way that God is happy with the things we say and do.

Ask: What can you do to please God?

- Place the shells within reach of the children.

- Encourage each child to name a way he or she can please God.

- After each child speaks, let the children place some shells in their jars. After the last child's turn, help the children put on their lids.

Say: The shell is a symbol for baptism.

- Encourage them to place their shell jars in their rooms to remind them of baptism.

Water Relay Race

Supplies: *bucket for each team, water, plastic cups*

Preparation:

- *At a running distance from each team, set a large bucket, filled with water.*

- Divide the children into two teams for a relay race.

- Give each child a plastic cup. Have the first child run down to the team's bucket and fill his or her cup with water. This child runs back to the line, tags the next child and goes to the back of the line with his or her cup of water.

- The child tagged runs and fills his or her cup with water, repeating the action of the child in front of him or her.

- Eventually all of the children on the team will have cups filled with water.

- Then, the child at the front of the line runs with his or her cup filled with water and pours it back into the bucket. He or she runs back and tags the next child in line.

- The tagged child runs and pours out the cup of water and runs back to tag the next child in line.

- The action is repeated until each child on a team has poured out his or her cup of water. The first team to do this wins the race.

 # We Worship God

Water Sounds

Supplies: *mats or rug, CD of water sounds, CD player; or tub filled with water, cup*

- Play a CD with water sounds or continuously dip and pour water using a cup in a tub of water.

- Let the children sit or lie down on mats or a rug.

- Encourage the children to close their eyes, relax and listen to the water sounds.

- As the music plays or as you dip and pour water, speak some quiet words to the children from time to time.

God loves you.
God is pleased with you.
God is happy with you.
Baptism is a happy time!
We baptize with water.
Sprinkling, pouring, immersion.
When we are baptized, God is with us.

Baptismal Dance

Supplies: *praise CD, CD player*

Say: In some countries, when a person is baptized, those at the baptism will dance to show their joy. Let's dance to show our love for God and to thank God for the gift of baptism.

- Play praise music. Have the children stand in a circle. Lead them in the following motions.

- Sway to the left and then to the right.

- Dance around in a circle.

- Step forward and step backward in the circle.

- Move around in a circle as clap your hands.

- Have everyone stand in a line and grab onto the shoulders of the person in front of them. Lead the children around the room.

- Let the children break free from the line and dance around the room.

Child of Promise, Child of Blessing

Supplies: Leaders' Guide—pp. 16-17, *bowl of water, plastic cup,* The United Methodist Hymnal *or CD of* The United Methodist Hymnal

Preparation:

- *Photocopy "A Note About Baptism" and "My Family Helps Me Worship" (pages 16-17) for each child.*

- Invite a singer in your congregation to sing *"Child of Blessing, Child of Promise"* (*The United Methodist Hymnal*, 611). Or play the hymn from the CD.

- As the hymn is sung, have each child come forward to your worship center.

- Scoop up water and drip it over the hand of each child as you call the child by name and say: You are a child of God. God loves you.

Pray: Thank you, God, for reaching out to us in our baptism. You know our names! Help us to please you, as Jesus did. Amen.

- Send "*A Note about Baptism*" and "*My Family Helps Me Worship*" home with each child.

 # A Note About Baptism

There are three methods of baptism practiced in The United Methodist Church: sprinkling, pouring, and immersion. Our church believes it is not the amount of water that is important. What is important is that God is present at all of our baptisms, no matter what age they occurred, in what settings, and what method was used.

In The United Methodist Church, we baptize infants because we believe that God's grace and love are extended to us from the moment of our birth. Believing parents bring their infants to be baptized in the midst of a caring congregation that vows to partner with parents in raising their child in the Christian faith.

At our baptism, God claims each of us as beloved children of God. God reaches out with grace and offers us the gift of God's abiding presence and unmerited love. In our Wesleyan tradition, we describe this powerful and decisive action of God as *prevenient grace*. God continually reaches out to us throughout our entire lives, seeking to draw us closer to our Creator. God is forever wooing us, even when we stray away from God or deny God with our thoughts and actions. In our baptism, the church affirms God's everlasting love for us.

If your child has been baptized, talk with him or her about the baptism. Show your child pictures. Tell the child about what he or she was wearing and who was present at the baptism. Show the child his or her baptismal certificate.

If your child has not been baptized, assure your child of God's love and faithfulness. If you have any questions about the sacrament of baptism, talk with your pastor.

 # My Family Helps Me Worship

Come to the Water—Baptism

Your child learned the Bible story about the baptism of Jesus by John the Baptist in the river Jordan. In this story, the child learned that God was pleased with Jesus and had the opportunity to explore ways that God is pleased with them today.

Talk Points for the Week

Ask: What are the three ways people are baptized in our church? *(sprinkling, pouring, and immersion)*

Ask: What is the symbol for baptism? *(shell)* for the Holy Spirit? *(dove)*

Ask: What are some of the things we can do to please God?

Family Worship Time

Set up a worship center in your home. Let the children in the family help you select a place for your worship center and items to place on your worship table.

How to Set Up Your Worship Center

1. Select a small table or card table.
2. Find a cloth to place on your center. Cover the worship center with the cloth. You might wish to select a white cloth. White is the liturgical color in the church used at baptisms.
3. Place some symbols on your table to represent the sacrament of baptism. Items you might include: shell, dove, and one white candle.
4. Add pictures of the baptism of family members and/or baptismal certificates.
5. Place a bowl of water on the table and a hand towel.

Worship God With Scripture

Read Matthew 3:16-17—Jesus Is Baptized.

Talk about the story of Jesus' baptism.

Ask: What is your the favorite part of the story?

Say: Imagine what it would have been like to observe the baptism of Jesus.

Share Baptismal Stories

If members of the family have been baptized, share some stories. After each story is shared say, "Remember your baptism, and be thankful."

Remind those members of the family who were baptized as infants that they can remember that God loved them when they were baptized and that other people loved them also.

Share Ways to Please God

Ask: What are some things we can do to please God?

After a family member shares a way to please God, have other family members present say, God is pleased.

Worship God With Songs

Sing some of your family's favorite hymns or praise choruses.

Your child learned that in some countries, people dance at a baptism as a way of praising God. Put on a CD of praise music, and dance!

Touch the Water and Bless

Have each family member dip his or her hands into the bowl of water on your worship table. As each family member touches the water, offer a blessing.

Say: You are a special child of God. God loves you, and God blesses you.

Pray: Thank you, God, for the gift of baptism. Thank you, God, for our family. Thank you, God, for our church. Thank you for this time to worship together as a family. Amen.

Come to the Table— Holy Communion

Bible Verse: After taking the bread and giving thanks, he broke it and gave it to them, saying, "This is my body, which is given for you. Do this in remembrance of me." (*Luke 22:19*)

Children will:

• Examine the Bible verse.

• Learn about the Passover Meal (Last Supper) Jesus shared with his disciples.

• Explore the meaning of Communion.

• Prepare to serve Communion to their congregation.

 # Worship Wisdom

Luke records for us the words of Jesus, spoken to his disciples at the Last Supper. Jesus and the disciples were gathered in an upper room in Jerusalem during the Jewish festival of Passover. Passover commemorated the pivotal event in the history of the Jewish nation, their deliverance from slavery in Egypt under the leadership of Moses.

Passover was usually observed in the home. Family and friends gathered to share in the remembrance. All of the food items eaten at Passover were symbolic of the sufferings of the Jewish people under the oppression of slavery imposed by the Egyptian pharaoh. Passover is a Jewish tradition that continues into the present time, as each year Jewish families gather to celebrate what is known as a seder meal. Jewish families today eat many of the same foods that Jesus ate at the Passover meal.

Christians sometimes refer to this meal as Jesus' Last Supper with his disciples. It was the last Passover meal Jesus ate with his followers before his crucifixion. During the meal, Jesus broke bread and referred to this bread as his broken body. He took a cup of wine and told his disciples that the cup represented his blood shed for them for the forgiveness of sins. Jesus took unleavened bread and one of the four cups of wine that were a part of the traditional Passover meal and

reinterpreted them to speak of his death on the cross. Jesus instructed his followers that whenever they gathered, they were to remember him by the breaking of bread and the sharing of the cup.

After the Passover meal, the Gospel writers tell us that Jesus went into the garden of Gethsemane, prayed, and submitted himself in full obedience to God. There he was arrested, later put on trial, and eventually crucified.

Christians observe Communion or the Lord's Supper as a way of remembering Jesus and his obedient sacrifice for each of us. We can teach our children to observe this special time in the church as a way to worship God. The observance of Communion also offers children an opportunity to thank God for Jesus, as they remember his steadfast obedience to God and his faithful trust in God. We must remember that children were not only included in Passover celebrations but also were given a significant role in the family meal. This tradition continues today in Passover observances. Just as children are important in Jewish Passover traditions, our children should be gladly welcomed to the table of our Lord. Children are a part of the family of God and must be joyfully invited to participate fully in the sacrament of Holy Communion.

Enter With Gladness

As the Children Arrive

Supplies: *a variety of breads*

- Greet each child by name. Tell each child that you are glad he or she is present.

- Have a variety of breads for the children to view. Tell the children from which countries your bread originated.

Taste the Bread

Supplies: *a variety of breads (Be aware of any allergies the children may have.)*

- Let the children taste the variety of breads.

Say: Today we are going to learn about Communion. Another name for Communion is the Lord's Supper. During Communion in our church, we eat bread. We remember Jesus. You are welcome to taste different kinds of bread from many parts of the world. All over the world, when people share in Communion, they use bread. When they eat the bread, they remember Jesus.

View the Worship Center

Supplies: *small table, white cloth, Bible, white candles, bread, Communion chalice, grapes*

Preparation:

- *Set up a Communion worship center. Place a white cloth (the liturgical color for Communion) on a small table.*

- *Place on the table a Bible, white candles, loaf of bread, Communion chalice, grapes, and other items that remind you of Communion.*

- Show the children the items on your worship center table.

Ask: What happens at Communion?

Bible Praise Notes

Share the Bible Story

Supplies: *Bible, picture of the Last Supper, picture of modern Communion (AbingdonPress.com/downloads)*

Preparation:

- *Download and print the pictures of the Last Supper and modern Communion.*

- Show the children where the story of Jesus' Last Supper is found in the Bible. (Luke 22:7-23)

- Point out that the story is found in all four of our Gospels: Matthew, Mark, Luke, and John. Tell or read the story of Jesus' Last Supper.

- Show the children the picture of Jesus and his disciples at the Last Supper and the picture of Communion being observed today.

- Let one child at a time come forward to point out people and elements in the picture.

Say: Find Jesus. Find bread. Find cups. Find one of Jesus' disciples. Find a person worshiping God and taking part in Communion. Find a minister.

Say: Jesus shared and his disciples shared a special meal called *Passover*. Today, we remember Jesus when we share a special time in our church where we eat bread and drink juice. We call this part of our worship service **Communion.**

Learn the Bible Verse

Supplies: *plastic bread or paper cutout of bread, music CD, CD player*

Preparation:

- *Provide plastic bread or cut a bread shape from construction paper.*

- Teach the children the Bible verse, Luke 22:19b (CEB) *"Eat this as a way of remembering me!"*

Say: These are the words Jesus said at the Last Supper. Today we remember Jesus when we share in Communion in our church.

- Have the children sit in a circle. Put on some music, and have the children pass the bread around the circle. Stop the music at intervals. The child holding the bread when the music stops will say the Bible verse.

- Once a child has a turn to say the Bible verse, if he or she is holding the bread when the music stops, ask that child holding the bread to pass the bread to another child who has not had a turn to say the Bible verse.

- Continue the game until all children have an opportunity to say the verse.

Bible Verse Puzzle

Supplies: *Reproducible 5—p. 100, scissors, envelopes*

Preparation:

- *Photocopy "Remember Jesus" (Reproducible 5) for each child.*

- Give each child "Remember Jesus." Have the children cut out the puzzle pieces. Let the children put their puzzle pieces together to form the Bible verse.

- Let children who can read help the younger children with their puzzles. Point out the words to the nonreaders. Let the children say the Bible verse several times.

- Give the children envelopes to put their puzzle pieces in to take home.

 # Let's Learn to Worship

Chalice and Bread

Supplies: *play dough, The United Methodist Hymnal or CD of Hymnal and CD player*

- Encourage the children to shape a loaf of bread and a chalice from play dough.

- As the children are shaping their loaf of bread and chalice, invite a singer in your church to sing for the children some Communion songs from *The United Methodist Hymnal*, 613-641, or play Communion songs from the CD.

All Are Welcome

Supplies: *pictures of person observing Communion representing different countries, races, ages, and gender. (AbingdonPress.com/download)*

Preparation:

- *Download and print the pictures of Communion.*

- Show the children the pictures. Let them identify who is observing Communion. After the children view each picture, have them shout together "All are welcome!"

Say: All are welcome to come for Communion, regardless of their age, the color of their skin, or whether they are male or female.

Eat This Bread

Supplies: The United Methodist Hymnal *or CD of hymnal and CD player*

- Teach the children "Eat This Bread," Hymn #628 in *The United Methodist Hymnal*.

- Teach them the following motions to use as they sing the hymn:

Eat this bread—pretend to eat bread

Drink this cup—pretend to drink

Come to me—move hands toward self

And never be hungry—move hands downward in a stiff, fast motion

Trust in me—clasp hands together

And you will not thirst—raise hands in the air

Make a Cloth for the Altar

Supplies: *white cloth,hemmed around the edges; paints; sponges in the shape of chalice, bread, heart, cross, church, or other religious shapes; smocks; washable paint*

- Give the children smocks to wear.

- Show them how to dip their sponges in paint and press on the white cloth.

- When dry, give the cloth to the pastor to use on Communion Sunday, or save to use for the Sunday that children serve Communion in the worship service.

Make a Communion Banner

Supplies: Reproducible 6—p. 101; purple, brown, and tan felt; dowel rods; yarn; scissors; glue; stapler; staples; ballpoint pens or felt-tip markers

Preparation:

- *Photocopy the "Chalice and Bread Patterns" (Reproducible 6) for each child.*

- Give each child brown felt and tan felt and the "Chalice and Bread Patterns." Have the children cut out the patterns.

- Help each child tape the chalice pattern onto the tan felt and the bread pattern onto the brown felt.

- Have the children trace around the patterns with a ballpoint pen or felt-tip marker. Let the children cut out the shapes.

- Give each child a piece of purple felt. Encourage the children to glue the chalice and bread onto the purple felt.

- Have each child turn the banner to the back. Help each child fold the top of the purple felt over the dowel, making a pocket. Glue or staple the pocket together. Tie yarn around each end of the dowel to make a hanger.

- Let the children take their banners home.

We Worship God

Seder Meal (Passover Meal)

Supplies: *pastor or other ordained elder; table; foods eaten at Passover (see next column), grapes, nuts, figs, and other biblical food; cushions; Bible-times costumes*

Preparation:

- *Invite your pastor to be present to share Communion with the children. If your pastor is not available, invite a retired ordained elder to be present.*

- *Set up a low table. Place cushions on the floor around the table.*

- *Display foods eaten during Passover.*

- Invite the children to sit around the table on the cushions. Have them recline on their left elbows during the meal.

- Let the children sample the foods. Share with the children what the foods symbolize.

Foods for the Seder Meal:

Bitter herbs – bitterness of slavery in Egypt

Parsley – springtime and new life

Unleavened bread – Jewish people didn't have time to let their bread rise in their haste to leave Egypt.

Water with salt – represents the tears of the Jewish people during their time of slavery

Haroset – a mixture of apples, raisins, cinnamon, honey, and nuts (recipe can be found online), represents the mortar used to make the bricks for Pharaoh's building projects. The Jewish people, as slaves, had to work very hard and build many building for the pharaoh.

- While the children are seated at the seder meal table, present the skit "Baking Bread in a Hurry!" to remind the children of the Exodus.

Say: The Passover meal Jesus shared with his disciples reminded the people that they had been set free from slavery. Another name for the Passover meal is the seder meal. Jewish people observe this meal with their families during Passover today.

- After the Passover meal, have the children share in Communion.

- Invite your pastor, another elder in your church, or a retired elder to consecrate the elements.

Say: Today we share Communion in our church to remember Jesus.

Baking Bread in a Hurry!

Characters: Two Jewish women named Hannah and Sarah, who are slaves in Egypt

Hannah: Welcome to my kitchen. My name is Hannah. I'm busy preparing bread for our family meal. I've put together all the ingredients for a delicious loaf of bread. All I have to do is add the yeast, then let the bread rise for several hours. After this, I will bake it in our oven. While I am kneading my bread, let me tell you my story. I am a Jewish woman and a slave in Egypt under the pharaoh. We have been slaves for all of my life. I have been praying to God for deliverance from slavery. Just the other day, a man named Moses approached the pharaoh and demanded that he let our people go free. I sure hope Moses can have some influence with the pharaoh. My husband has to work long hours making bricks for the pharaoh's large building projects. Pharaoh is always building larger and larger monuments to himself.

Children: Sing to the tune of "Here We Go Round the Mulberry Bush"

This is the way we knead our bread,
knead our bread, knead our bread.
This is the way we knead our bread,
so early in the morning.

Sarah: *(rushing in excitedly):* Hannah, great news! Moses has convinced the pharaoh to let us go free! Moses said we must hurry and pack all of our belongings. We must be ready to go soon. He says to prepare as much food as possible to take on our journey!

Hannah: Praise the Lord! We will be free at last!

Sarah: Let me help you prepare some food for the journey. We'll get very hungry in the wilderness. What about the bread? Is it ready?

Hannah: No, there's no yeast in it, so it won't rise.

Sarah: We don't have time to add yeast! We'll just bake it when we reach a resting place in our travels. Never mind that our bread will be flat. What is important is that we have some bread to eat on our long journey.

Hannah: You're right sister. I'll begin packing the unleavened bread right now!

Children: Sing to the tune of "Here We Go Round the Mulberry Bush"

This is the way we bake our bread
bake our bread, bake our bread.
This is the way we bake our bread,
so early in the morning.

This is the way we thank our God,
thank our God, thank our God.
This is the way we thank our God,
so early in the morning.

Hannah/Sarah: Sing to the tune of "Here We Go Round the Mulberry Bush."

Moses came to set us free,
set us free, set us free.
Moses came to set us free,
so early in the morning.

We are leaving Egypt soon,
Egypt soon, Egypt soon.
We are leaving Egypt soon,
and God will lead the way.

There is no time for bread to rise,
bread to rise, bread to rise.
There is no time for bread to rise,
flat bread will have to do.

Children Serve Communion

Supplies: *Leaders' Guide—p. 23-24*, pastor, *large piece of cloth, chalice, Communion plate, grapes in a basket, cross, Communion altar cloth made by the children (see page 21), and other items that symbolize Communion*

Preparation:

- *Photocopy "A Note About Communion" and "My Family Helps Me Worship" (pp. 23-24) for each child.*

- Speak with your pastor and other worship leaders to gain their approval for the children to serve Communion in your worship service. Assure your adult leaders that the children will be trained. Select a date for the children to serve Communion.

- Select four children to carry in the large piece of cloth. Have the four children hold each end of the cloth. They will process into the sanctuary and bring the cloth to the front.

- Select other children to carry in the Communion items. These children will process into the sanctuary. As each child approaches the children holding the cloth, these children will lift up the cloth into the air. The child holding the Communion item will walk under the cloth. After the child walks under the cloth, the children will bring the cloth back down. This action will be repeated as each child processes in, carrying a Communion item.

- Each child will go to the Communion table and place his or her item on the table.

- Have the child with the Communion cloth come in first so he or she can cover the Communion table before the other items are brought into the sanctuary and placed on the Communion table. If you do not choose to use the Communion altar cloth made by the children, select another cloth to place on the table.

- Select other children to serve Communion. Show them where to stand in the sanctuary, and instruct them on what to say as each person comes to take the bread and cup.

- Invite your pastor to be present to teach the children.

Pray: Thank you, God, for the time in our church when we remember Jesus. We are happy to share in Communion. Thank you for the bread that we eat and the juice that we drink. Thank you that all are welcome to share in Communion in our church. Amen.

- Send home *"A Note About Communion"* and *"My Family Helps Me Worship."*

A Note About Communion

The Last Supper was actually the Passover meal that Jesus celebrated with his disciples. This special meal reminded the children of Israel about their deliverance from slavery in Egypt. All of the foods eaten at the Passover, or seder, meal helped the people recall the bitterness of slavery and the joyful deliverance by Moses, their leader.

Communion is a special time in our church. An ordained elder always blesses the Communion elements, although laity may serve the elements of bread and juice to the congregation. Communion is one of two sacraments in our church, the other being baptism.

Children are welcome to participate in Holy Communion because in the Jewish tradition,

Passover was and is a family celebration. Our Communion ritual stems from the Passover celebration because at the Last Supper Jesus took bread and wine and reinterpreted these elements to speak of his sacrifice on the cross. Since children are an essential part of the family of God, they must be welcome to come to the table.

All people are welcome to participate in Communion in The United Methodist Church, regardless of age, gender, or race. Jesus invites each of us to come to the table of grace. At the table of our Lord, which is a table of grace and hospitality, all are equal and all are welcome. However, it is essential that we come to the table with a penitent heart, a confessing spirit, and a humble attitude.

 # My Family Helps Me Worship

Come to the Table—Holy Communion:

Your child has learned about Communion in our United Methodist tradition. He or she also learned about Jesus' Last Supper with his disciples. This was a Passover meal that reminded the children of Israel about their deliverance from slavery in Egypt. All of the foods eaten at the Passover, or Seder, meal helped the people recall the bitterness of slavery and the joyful deliverance by Moses, their leader. Your child was able to taste some of the Passover foods. Many of these foods are the same ones eaten by the Jewish people today as they celebrate Passover every year in their homes.

Talk Points for the Week

Ask: Who do we remember at Communion? *(Jesus)*

Ask: Who can take Communion in the church? *(all)*

Ask: What food do we eat during Communion? *(bread)* What do we drink? *(grape juice)*

Family Worship

Set up a worship center in your home. Let the children in the family help you select a place for your worship center and find items to place on your worship table.

How to Set Up Your Worship Center

1. Select a small table or card table.

2. Find a cloth to place on your table. You might wish to select a white cloth. White is the liturgical color in the church used for Communion.

3. Place some symbols on your table to represent the sacrament of Communion. Items might include: bread, chalice, cross, juice.

Worship God With Scripture

Read Luke 22:14-20—The Last Supper.

Share About Communion

Let family members take turns lifting up a loaf of bread and the chalice. When they lift them up, ask them to share about their favorite part of Communion in church. As each person shares, have other family members respond with the words, "Eat this as a way of remembering Jesus."

Share in a Communion Litany
Remember Me!

Leader: Jesus and his disciples gathered in the upper room to share in the Last Supper.

All: **Jesus said, "Remember me."**

Leader: Jesus took bread and broke it.

All: **Jesus said, "Remember me."**

Leader: Jesus took a cup and lifted it and let his disciples drink.

All: **Jesus said, "Remember me."**

Leader: Jesus and his disciples sang a hymn and left the Upper Room.

All: **Jesus said, "Remember me."**

Leader: We remember Jesus when we take Communion in our church.

All: **Jesus said, "Remember me."**

Pray: Thank you God for Communion. Thank you God for our family. Thank you God for our church. Thank you for this time to worship together as a family. Amen

Share Communion With Others

Ask family members to think of someone outside of the family that they would like to share Communion with in your church. Invite that person to sit with the family in the worship service when Communion is served, and go to the altar together as friends in Christ.

Worship Leaders Help Children Praise God

Bible Verse: He gave some apostles, some prophets, some evangelists, and some pastors and teachers. His purpose was to equip God's people for the work of serving and building up the body of Christ. (*Ephesians 4:11-12*)

Children will:

- Examine the Bible verses.
- Identify worship leaders in their own church.
- Learn about the roles and tasks of worship leaders.
- Consider ways to show appreciation to their church worship leaders.

 # Worship Wisdom

The Book of Ephesians lists for us some of the worship leaders in the early church. Many people credit the authorship of the book to the apostle Paul, while others believe that another author wrote the Book of Ephesians. Regardless, this writer seeks to strengthen and confirm believers in their faith and remind them of the vital role of worship leaders, who are called by God for specific tasks.

The worship leaders mentioned in Ephesians are identified as the offices of *apostles, prophets, evangelists, preachers,* and *teachers.* All of these leaders were called by God to equip the worshipers in their service to God and others. The worship leaders were also selected by God to build up the body of Christ in unity, grace, and love. These were important tasks that required dedicated leaders and supportive followers.

Apostles were special individuals chosen by Christ who were witnesses to the resurrection of Jesus. The twelve disciples were also called apostles in the early church, along with the apostle Paul, due to his unique experience on the Damascus road.

A *prophet* is a messenger of God who diligently studies the Scriptures, looks critically at the world around him or her, and testifies of things to come,

based upon the minds, hearts, and actions of the people.

An *evangelist* preaches the word of God wherever he or she is sent in the world. While we no longer have apostles in our churches, there are some individuals who have the gift of *prophecy.* Others are called to be *evangelists, preachers,* and *teachers.*

As you help the children identify worship leaders in your own church, remind them that, like the worship leaders in the early church, your leaders today are chosen by God and given their gifts under the leadership and guidance of the Holy Spirit. And like the early church worship leaders, competent and good leaders today direct us in our worship of God and teach us ways to grow in our faith.

Church leaders help us identify our own unique gifts and encourage us to use these gifts in service. Under their leadership, our churches are challenged to grow in our love and unity for each other, our community, and the world. Qualified leaders provide us examples of Christlike living that we can emulate.

Enter With Gladness

As the Children Arrive

Supplies: *digital camera; laptop; or printer, photo paper, tape*

Preparation:

• *Take pictures of key worship leaders including your pastor(s), choir director, minister of music, organist, pianist, head usher, director/minister of children's ministries, youth director/minister, director of praise band, hand bell director, and other worship leaders.*

• *Enlarge and print the pictures for display on the classroom walls.*

• *Place the pictures at different places around your classroom walls. Or download these pictures and show them to the children on a laptop.*

• Greet each child by name. As each child enters, express gladness that he or she is present.

• Direct the child's attention to the pictures of the worship leaders in your church. Or, if you are using a laptop to show the pictures, have this running as the children arrive.

• Let each child take a few minutes to walk around and look at the pictures or view the pictures on the laptop.

• Let the children tell you the names of the worship leaders and what they do in worship. Help the children they are if unfamiliar with a name or a worship role.

Say: These are pictures of worship leaders in our church. Today we'll learn about worship leaders and what they do to help us worship.

Who Does What?

Supplies: Reproducible 7—p. 102, *pencils*

Preparation:

• *Photocopy "Worship Leaders" (Reproducible 7) for each child.*

• Give each child "Worship Leaders." Have the children draw a line from the worship leader to the item he or she uses in worship.

• Let the children share why each item goes with that worship leader or his or her leadership role seen in the pictures.

View the Worship Center

Supplies: *Bible, hymnal, stole, bulletin, acolyte lighter, choir anthem, musical pieces for the organ, music notes, small piano, offering plate*

Preparation:

• *Set up a worship center on a small table. Cover the table with a cloth.*

• *Place on the table some items that represent your worship leaders.*

• Show the children the items on your worship table. Pick up each item and ask the children to identify the person in your church who uses that item. Be sure and share his or her name with the children, along with title and or worship role.

Bible Praise Notes

Learn the Bible Verses

Supplies: *Bible*

• Show the children where the Bible verses are found in the Bible. Read the Bible verses.

Say: These are the names of some of the worship leaders in the early church.

• Let the children repeat after you the titles of the offices of the worship leaders mentioned in Ephesians 4:11.

26

- Have them practice saying each title several times. Then let them say all of the titles, one after the other.

Say: Today we have pastors, teachers, and evangelists, just like the early church. No matter what name we give our worship leaders, God gives these leaders gifts so that they can help us grow in our faith. They help our church members love each other and serve others. They remind us of the gifts that God gives each of us. They help us use our gifts to worship God and to serve our church.

A Visit from Early Church Leaders

Supplies: *Bible-times costumes*

Preparation:

- *Select individuals to play the role of an apostle, a prophet, an evangelist, a pastor, and a teacher.*

- *Dress them in biblical costumes and have them share with the children.*

- The following are suggested scripts to use.

Apostle

I am an apostle named Peter. You might remember my name because I was a disciple of Jesus. Before I became a disciple, I was a fisherman. After following Jesus as a disciple, I became a leader in the early church. Not everyone could be an apostle. Only the disciples of Jesus and those who had seen the resurrection of Jesus could be called an apostle. I help teach the people about Jesus and I preach about Jesus so the people will not forget him. Since I was a disciple of Jesus, I can give a firsthand account of what it was like to travel with Jesus, witness his miracles, and hear him teach.

Prophet

I am a prophet named Zebedee. Prophets are talked about both in the Old Testament and New Testament. A prophet carefully studies the Scriptures and tries to help the people understand what God wants them to do. I remind the people what will happen to them in the future because I understand Scripture and I pray to God for guidance. I try to guide the people in our churches to do what is right and follow God's ways.

Evangelist

I am an evangelist named Thaddeus. An evangelist preaches the word of God. I travel all over the country and preach in many different places. Today, there are evangelists who travel all over the world, preaching about Jesus.

Pastor

I am pastor John. I preach and teach the people in my congregation. I am their leader. Today, you have a pastor in your church. He or she preaches and teaches God's Word and instructs the people in your church about God's way of living. I hope that you listen carefully to your pastor. He or she wants to help you grow in your faith and use your gifts to serve God.

Teacher

My name is Priscilla and I am a teacher, along with my husband Aquila. The church where we teach actually meets in our home, rather than a church building like you worship in today. We are friends of the apostle Paul. He asked us to teach the people about Jesus. We hold Bible studies and worship services in our home, and many people attend. Our home is often crowded with men, women, and children who want to learn about Jesus and worship God. In your church, you are blessed with many teachers. Your worship leaders are teachers, along with your Sunday school teachers. Your worship leaders teach you through music, preaching, and all that they do in your worship service. Watch these worship leaders, and listen carefully to them. If you do, you will learn much to help you grow in your faith.

Scripture Worship Leader Cheer

Supplies: *pompoms, one for each child*

- Give each child a pompom. You can order inexpensive pompoms online from novelty stores.

- After each title is named, have the children shake their pompoms and say, "Thanks be to God!"

Say: Give me an apostle!
Give me a prophet!
Give me an evangelist!
Give me a pastor!
Give me a teacher!

Let's Learn to Worship

My Prayer Booklet

Supplies: *construction paper, plain paper, stapler, staples, markers, glue, scissors, optional: stickers*

Preparation:

- *Make prayer booklets for each child. Use construction paper, folded in half, for the cover and several sheets of 8½- by-11 inch pieces of plain paper, folded in half, for the inside of the booklet.*

- *Attach the cover to the white sheets of paper with a stapler.*

- *Photocopy (with each person's permission) the pictures you took of your worship leaders. Each child will need a set of pictures.*

- Give each child a prayer booklet and a set of the pictures of your worship leaders.

- Have the children cut out the pictures of the worship leaders and glue them into the booklet, one picture on each page.

- Have the children decorate the outside of their booklets by drawing worship symbols or using stickers.

- Have the children draw symbols by the pictures of each of the worship leaders to remind the children of what that worship leader does in the service. For example, the children could draw a Bible by the picture of their pastor or a music note by the picture of a music leader.

- Write the names of the worship leaders on a dry erase board or piece of poster paper. Help the children write the names of each worship leader by his or her picture. Have volunteers write for younger children.

- Encourage the children to place one of their hands over each picture as you say a sentence prayer for each worship leader by name.

Say: Thank you God for Pastor _____.

- Have the children repeat your prayer.

Say: Thank you God for our organist _____.

- Have the children repeat your prayer.

- Continue until prayers have been said for all worship leaders.

- Encourage the children to take their prayer booklets home and pray for the worship leaders. Encourage them to show their booklets to family members who can help them with the names of worship leaders.

Invite Acolytes

Supplies: *acolyte robes, candles, candlelighters*

- Invite some of your older acolytes to share with the children about their role as worship leaders. Let the acolytes wear their robes.

- Let the acolytes show the children how they light the candles and put out the light after the worship service is over.

- Let other children present in your worship session who are acolytes also share.

Make a Stole for Your Pastor

Supplies: Reproducibles 24-25—pp. 119-120, *scissors, cardboard, white cloth hemmed in shape of a stole (Ask your pastor to lend you a stole, if he or she has one, so you can obtain an accurate measurement.), paint pens, masking tape, smocks*

Preparation:

- *Use the symbols (Reproducibles 24-25) to make stencils out of cardboard.*

- *Borrow several different color stoles from a pastor to show the children.*

Say: Some ministers wear stoles around their necks during the worship service. The stole reminds us that the pastor has been chosen by God to be a minister. Ministers wear stoles as a symbol that they are serving Jesus and seeking to obey Jesus. Ministers wear a different color stole at different times in our church year. *(Hold up the different stoles.)*

- Have the children wear smocks.

- Use masking tape to secure the stole to your work surface and keep it from slipping.

- Let each child have a turn at tracing a religious symbol on the stole.

- If you have a large group of children, you may wish to decorate several stoles and give them to other ordained ministers on your staff or to retired ordained ministers.

Sing and Serve

Supplies: *slips of paper, pencil, basket or bag*

Preparation:

- *Write on slips of paper some ways that children can serve as worship leaders.*

- *Put the slips of paper in a basket or bag.*

- Select a child to draw out a slip of paper and read it out loud. If a child drawing out a slip of paper is not a reader, whisper to him or her what is written and have him or her repeat what you whisper to the other children.

- When a child reads a way children can serve as worship leaders, have the children sing the praise chorus: *Praise God, Praise God, All Ye Little Children* with the following words:

Serve God, serve God,
all ye little children.
God is love, God is love.
Serve God, serve God,
all ye little children.
God is love, God is love.

- Continue to draw out slips of paper and sing until all the slips of paper are drawn.

Some suggestions are:

Acolyte

Read Scripture

Sing in the children's choir

Play in the children's hand bell choir

Usher

Pass out bulletins

Make Thank-You Cards

Supplies: *markers, buttons, ribbons, small dried flowers, construction paper*

- Give each child a piece of construction paper. Instruct the children to fold their paper in half to make a card.

- Give each child the name of a worship leader. Be sure that each worship leader in your church gets a card.

- Encourage the children write a note of thanks inside the card or draw a picture. Write the words "Thank you" inside the card for younger children.

- Have the children decorate the outside of their cards by gluing on buttons, ribbons, and/or dried flowers.

- Present the cards to worship leaders.

Worship Leader Appreciation

Supplies: *party decorations, refreshments, invitations, posterboard, crayons or markers, tape*

- Let the children plan an appreciation tea and art show for worship leaders.

- Select a date.

- Inform parents.

- Invite worship leaders.

- Let the children decorate the room with streamers and other decorations.

- Serve cupcakes/cookies and punch/tea.

- Have small gifts, such as bookmarks for the worship leaders.

- Let the children sing some songs, read a poem, or read notes of appreciation they have written.

- Have each child draw a picture about worship on the posterboard Display the pictures and the tea becomes an art show.

We Worship God

Lead a Worship Service

Supplies: Preparation:

- *Photocopy "Outline of Worship Service" (p. 31) for each child.*

- *Set up your room similar to the way you worship in the sanctuary.*

- *Use benches for pews or sit in chairs, whichever is the tradition in your church.*

- *Use a small table for an altar. Cover your table with the altar cloth the children made in the session on Communion.*

- *Place on the table candles, a cross, the Bible, and some small baskets for offering plates.*

- *Borrow the acolyte lighter used in your church.*

- Invite the children to assume leadership roles during your time of worship.

Suggestions for Leadership Roles

Acolytes—light altar candles

Ushers—take up offering

Greeters—greet other children as they arrive for worship

Scripture Readers—read the passage from Ephesians 4:11-12 and other short Bible readings: select third-graders who are good readers

Song Leader—introduce the songs the children will sing

Liturgist—lead in call to worship: select a reader

Liturgist—offer a prayer: select a child who does not object to saying a public prayer

Liturgist—give the benediction: select a reader

Rehearse

- Have adult volunteers briefly rehearse with the children their parts in the worship service.

- Show the children where they need to stand in the worship service.

- While these children are rehearsing, let the other children select some praise songs they wish to sing in the worship service. Let your song leader be present to hear the children's suggestions. Let the children sing their praise songs as you wait for the other children to return.

- Give each child some play money to use for his or her offering during the worship service.

- Give each child a tambourine to play as you enter the "sanctuary." Walk to the "sanctuary" singing a praise song.

- Have the greeters stationed at the entrance to your "sanctuary" to greet the children.

Outline of Worship Service

Acolytes Light the Candles

Call to Worship Litany—Have the children shake their tambourine when they say "Thank you God."

> Leader: We thank God for worship leaders!
>
> **All: Thank you God!**
>
> Leader: We thank God for our pastor!
>
> **All: Thank you God!**
>
> Leader: We thank God for our music leaders!
>
> **All: Thank you God!**
>
> Leader: We thank God for our ushers!
>
> **All: Thank you God!**
>
> Leader: We thank God for acolytes!
>
> **All: Thank you God!**

Praise Songs—Sing some praise songs. Let your song leader ask the children to stand as they sing. Let him or her tell the children which song they will sing. Have the children shake their tambourines as they sing.

Prayer

Scripture Reading—Read Ephesians 4:11-12.

Sharing About What We Learned—Let the children share some of the things they learned about worship leaders in the early church and today. Choose a child to read the questions and encourage all the children to answer.

Ask: What were some of the leaders in the early church called? *(apostles, prophets, evangelists, teachers, pastors)*

Ask: Who are some of our worship leaders in the church today? What do they do?

Ask: How do worship leaders help us? *(recognize our gifts, provide unity, show love)*

Ask: What is the name of what some pastors wears around their necks in worship? *(stole)*

Ask: What are some things children can do in worship to serve as worship leaders? *(acolyte, read Scripture, usher, greet, sing in children's choir, play hand bells)*

Offering—Have the ushers pass the offering plates and let the children put in their play money.

Acolytes Extinguish Candles and Carry Out the Light

Benediction:

> Go in peace. Go to love others. Go as a child of God. Amen.

(Have children join hands as you share the closing prayer.)

Prayer: Thank you, God, for our worship leaders. They teach us about God and help us grow in our faith. Help us listen carefully to our worship leaders and show them love and respect. Amen.

• *Photocopy "My Family Helps Me Worship" (p. 32) and send a copy home with each child.*

My Family Helps Me Worship

Worship Leaders Help Children Praise God

Your child learned about worship leaders in the early church and in our church today. Some of the early church leaders we discussed were apostles, prophets, evangelists, pastors, and teachers. We explored with the children the Scripture verses *"He gave some apostles, some prophets, some evangelists, and some pastors and teachers. His purpose was to equip God's people for the work of serving and building up the body of Christ."* (Ephesians 4:11-12)

Talk Points for the Week

Ask: Who were some of the worship leaders in the early church? *(apostles, prophets, evangelists, pastors, and teachers)*

Ask: What did they do to help people worship?

Ask: Who are some of the worship leaders in our church?

Ask: What do they do to help people worship?

Family Worship

Set up a worship center in your home. Let the children in the family help you find select a place for your worship center and items to place on your worship table.

How to Set Up Your Worship Center

1. Select a small table or card table.

2. Find a cloth to place on your table. You might wish to select a cloth that is the color of the liturgical season in the church.

3. Place the prayer booklet your child made with pictures of worship leaders on your worship table.

4. Prior to the worship service, let your child help you cut out hearts from red construction paper. Cut out hearts equal to the number of the worship leaders in your child's prayer booklet.

Worship God With Scripture

Read: *Ephesians 4:11-12*

Read the verses again and pause when you get to the words *apostles, prophets, evangelists, pastors,* and *teachers.* Let the family members shout out the names.

Read the verses again and when you read the words "for the work of serving," have family members put their hands on top of each other in a circle.

Read the verses again and when you read the words, "building up the body of Christ," have family members put their palms upward and lift in the air as if they were lifting a heavy weight.

Sing a Praise Song About Worship Leaders

Sing to the tune of "Are You Sleeping?"

Thank you, thank you.
Thank you, thank you.
Pastor (insert name of pastor),
Pastor (insert name of pastor,)
Thank you for your service.
Thank you for your service.
We love you.

Continue singing, changing each verse to reflect a different worship leader: "Mr./Mrs. (name of usher, musician, acolyte, and so forth)."

Prayers and Blessings for Worship Leaders

Open your child's prayer booklet. As you view the picture of each worship leader, have family members lay their hands on top of the picture and offer a prayer. Place one of the hearts on the picture of the worship leader as a sign of your love and appreciation.

Pray: Thank you, God, for our church worship leaders. Thank you for the gifts and talents you have given each of them. Thank you for the ways they help us worship God. Be with them. Bless them with the peace of Christ. Amen.

5 Church Symbols Help Children Worship God

Bible Verse: This will be a symbol among you. In the future your children may ask, "What do these stones mean to you?" *Joshua 4:6*

Children will:
• Examine the Bible verse.

• Identify symbols in worship.

• Learn the meaning of certain symbols.

• Think about the importance of symbols in worship.

 Worship Wisdom

Read Joshua 4.

Joshua, chapter four, tells the vivid story of the crossing of the Jordan River under the leadership of Joshua. Moses had died, leaving Joshua as the new leader of the Israelites. God gave Joshua the awesome task of leading the children of Israel into the Promised Land.

As the people crossed the Jordan River, God instructed Joshua to select twelve men, representing the twelve tribes of Israel. Each representative was to take one large stone out of the Jordan River and carry it to the campground of the Jewish people. Joshua also placed twelve stones in the Jordan River to mark the spot where God aided the travelers.

Joshua told the people that the stones in the river and the stones in their camp were symbols or signs pointing to God's faithfulness. God had helped them enter the Promised Land. God held back the waters so the people could cross the Jordan River. In a similar way God held back the waters of the Red Sea when the people left Egypt. In our story, the priests were able to safely carry the chest containing the covenant (Ark of the Covenant) that contained the Ten Commandments and represented the presence of God.

Furthermore, the stones provided a powerful symbol for the children. When children looked at the stones, they would ask questions about their meaning. This would provide an opportunity for the adults to share with the young people about God's faithful actions in the past and God's continued love and mercy in the present and future.

Like the twelve stones, worship symbols today help our children learn about God. Joshua was certain that the symbols of stones would pique the interest of the children, and they would be motivated to ask questions. The symbols presented an opportunity to teach about God.

Today, children see your worship symbols. And like the children of Joshua's time, your children ask questions about the meaning of these symbols. Their probing questions give you an opportunity to share with them about the wondrous works of God, just as the people of Joshua's time used their symbols to speak of God's power and might.

Enter With Gladness

As the Children Arrive

- Greet each child by name. As each child enters, express gladness that he or she is present.

Symbols Worksheet

Supplies: Reproducible 8—p. 103, *pencils, crayons*

Preparation:

- *Photocopy "Worship Symbols" (Reproducible 8) for each child.*

- Give each child "Worship Symbols." *Secure volunteers to help nonreaders.*

- Have the children draw a line from each symbol to its meaning.

- The children may color their symbols.

Visit the Worship Center

Supplies: *small table, cloth, Bible, candle, cross, crown, offering plate, Christian flag, American flag, cross and flame, heart, lily, butterfly, chalice, loaf of bread*

Preparation:

- *Set up a worship center. Cover a table with a cloth.*

- *Place some worship symbols on the table.*

Ask: What event do you think of when you see a Christmas tree? *(Christmas)* colored eggs? *(Easter)* hearts? *(Valentine's Day)* an American flag? *(our country, patriotism)*

Say: Our church has many symbols that help us think of God and God's love.

- Show the children the symbols on your table. Talk with the children about each symbol and what it stands for in the church.

Bible Praise Notes

Learn the Bible Story

Supplies: *Bible, small inflatable or plastic swimming pool, water, newspaper or plastic bags, grocery bags, tape, small tent and camping gear, volunteer to play Joshua, Bible-times costume*

Preparation:

- *Set up a small inflatable or plastic swimming pool with water in it to represent the Jordan River. Supervise children at all times.*

- *Make twelve stones by stuffing newspaper into brown grocery bags and secure with tape. Place the stones around the outside of the pool.*

- *Set up the campground of the children of Israel using a small tent and some camping gear.*

- *Select a person to play the role of Joshua. Ask him or her to tell the story "Twelve Stones" (p.35) Provide a Bible-times costume for him to wear.*

- Gather the children around the Jordan River.

- Show the children where the Book of Joshua is found in the Bible.

Say: Joshua was the leader of the children of Israel after the death of Moses. The people had wandered in the wilderness for many years. Now it was time to enter the land promised by God. But the people had to cross the Jordan River to enter the Promised Land.

- Encourage the children to pretend to be a part of the group that crossed the Jordan River.

Say: God helped the people cross the Jordan River. The people carried the chest containing

the covenant with them. This was a container for the Ten Commandments. The people rejoiced when they arrived safely on the shore and they were very happy that the chest containing the covenant arrived unharmed.

- Introduce Joshua to the children. Encourage the children to say, What do these stones mean? whenever Joshua says the word "stone".

Twelve Stones

It was time to enter the Promised Land! But the River Jordan was in our way. It was too deep! We could not safely cross the deep river. But God showed us the way.

God told me to have the men carrying the chest containing the covenant to step into the river. When their feet touched the river the water stopped flowing! Everyone could cross over the river by walking on the dry riverbed.

God told me to select one man out of each of our twelve tribes to pick up a **stone** (children respond: "What do these stones mean?") from the Jordan River and carry the **stone** (children respond: "What do these stones mean?") to our campground.

The **stones** (children respond: "What do these stones mean?") are symbols from God. They remind us that God helped us cross the Jordan River.

When we look at the **stones** ("children respond: What do these stones mean?") we remember that God loves us.

God wants our children to look at the **stones** (children respond: What do these stones mean?) and learn about God. We must teach our children about God's love and kindness!

- Have Joshua select twelve children, one at a time. As each child is selected, he or she is to go to the Jordan River, select a stone, and take it to the campground. Have each child pretend like the stone is very heavy and hard to carry.

- If you have fewer than twelve children present, give each child an extra turn. You can pair children together to ensure each child is given an extra turn.

- Have the children sing these words to the tune of "We are Climbing Jacob's Ladder."

> We are crossing Jordan River.
> We are crossing Jordan River.
> We are crossing Jordan River,
> children of the Lord.
>
> God is with us on our journey.
> God is with us on our journey.
> God is with us on our journey,
> children of the Lord.
>
> Stones are symbols of God's mercy.
> Stones are symbols of God's mercy.
> Stones are symbols of God's mercy,
> children of the Lord.

- After all the stones are placed at the campground, have the children gather there.

- **Have them say: "What do these stones mean?"**

- **Have Joshua respond: "These stones are symbols of God's love."**

- Have twelve other children return the stones to the Jordan River.

- Repeat the exercise until all children have a chance to carry a stone either from the Jordan River to the campground or from the campground to the Jordan River.

God Stones

Supplies: *smooth stones, red markers*

- Give each child a smooth stone. Help him or her write the word "GOD" on one side of the stone with a marker.

- On the other side, have the children draw a heart.

Say: You have drawn a symbol on your rock. This symbol, the heart, is to remind you of God's love.

Let's Learn to Worship

Worship Symbol Clings

Supplies: Reproducibles 24-25—pp. 119-120, *plastic sandwich bags, scissors, fabric paint, paper plates*

Preparation:

- *Photocopy the symbols (Reproducibles 24-25) for each child.*

- Give each child the worship symbols patterns and scissors. Have the children cut out the symbols.

- Identify each of the symbols with the children.

- Have the children choose one of the symbols to make a cling.

- Give each child a paper plate. Have the child write his or her name on the plate.

- Give each child a plastic bag. Place the bag flat on each paper plate.

- Show each child how to place the symbol pattern so it is facing up inside the plastic bag.

- Encourage the children to use fabric paint to fill in the spaces on the design. Do not leave holes.

- Set the painted symbols aside to dry until the next session (at least 24 hours).

- After the clings are dry, show the children how to peel off the designs from the plastic bags. The clings will stick to windows and other surfaces.

Visit the Sanctuary

- Take the children on a tour of the sanctuary. Point out the symbols in each sanctuary.

- If your church has stained-glass windows, let the children look at the symbols in the window.

- Invite a person in your congregation, familiar with the symbols in your windows, to share with the children what each symbol means.

Missing Symbol

Supplies: *worship center prepared earlier*

- Gather the children around your worship center and have them take a close look at the symbols.

- Have the children sit down on the floor. Instruct them to turn around so they are not facing the worship center.

- Remove one symbol from the worship center.

- Have the children turn around. The first child to raise his or her hand and correctly identify the missing symbol gets to remove another symbol from the worship center.

- Continue the game until all of the symbols have been hidden at least once.

Stained-Glass Butterflies

Supplies: *wax paper, crayon shavings (shaved with a scissor or knife by an adult), scissors, iron, hole punch, yarn*

Say: The butterfly is a symbol we often see in the spring. It reminds us that Jesus is alive!

- Give each child a piece of wax paper. Have him or her fold the wax paper in half.

- Show the children how to draw half a butterfly on the wax paper with the body at the fold.

- Show the children how to flip the wax paper over and draw the other half of the butterfly, so the two sides of the butterfly match.

- Have each child unfold his or her wax paper and put it on a flat surface.

- Put some crayon shavings on the wax paper of each child, inside the butterfly shape.

- Give each child another piece of wax paper and place this on top of the other sheet of wax paper on which the child has drawn the butterfly.

- Have an adult iron the two layers of wax paper together on low heat.

- After the drawings are ironed, let each child cut out his or her stained-glass butterfly.

- Punch a hole near the top. Tie a piece of yarn in the hole for hanging.

Signs and Symbols

Supplies: Reproducibles 24-25—pp. 119-120, *scissors, paper plates, glitter crayons or glitter glue, pencils, craft sticks, tape*

Preparation:

- *Photocopy the symbols (Reproducibles 24-25) for each child.*

- Let the children enjoy this activity while another adult is ironing the butterflies.

- Give each child the worship symbols patterns. Have the children cut out the symbols.

- Give each child a paper plate. Let the child use a pencil to choose a symbol and trace it in the center of the paper plate. Encourage the children to choose different symbols so that all the symbols are represented.

- Have the children turn their paper plates to the back. Have each child write his or her name on the back of the plate. Help each child tape a craft stick to the back of the paper plate to make a handle.

- Turn the plates over to the front.

- Encourage the children to outline their symbol tracings with glitter crayons or glitter glue.

- Plan to use the signs and symbols during "We Worship God."

The Meaning of Symbols Game

- Divide the children into two teams. Have the two teams form a line, one child after the other.

- The first child in line on team one goes to the worship center and holds up a symbol for team two to view.

- The first child in line on team two should give the meaning of the symbol. If that child gives the correct answer, he or she may go to the worship center to hold up another symbol for team one to guess its meaning.

- The child on team one who held up the symbol moves to the back of the line, so that the next child in line on team one can tell the meaning of the symbol.

- Keep playing the game until all children have a turn at telling what the symbol means.

 # We Worship God

Butterflies and Music

Supplies: *praise music CD, CD player, stained-glass butterflies made earlier*

- Play some praise music. Let the children move their stained-glass butterflies to the music.

- Let the children walk around in a circle waving their stained-glass butterflies.

- Let the children march with a partner as they wave their stained-glass butterflies.

- Have the children form a line and gently bob their stained-glass butterflies on their hands, as they walk.

- Have the children form a line, and let the children walk by the worship table. As each child approaches the table, have him or her stop and wave the stained-glass butterfly over the symbols on the worship table.

Body Sculptures

Supplies: Reproducibles 24-25—pp. 119-120, *scissors*

Preparation:

- *Photocopy the symbols (Reproducibles 24-25) for the children. You will need a symbol for each small group.*

- Divide the children into small groups.

- Give each group a worship symbol. Have each group make sure that no other groups can see its symbol.

- Instruct the groups to find a way to show their symbol using only their bodies to form "body sculptures." They may not make any sounds or spell out any words.

- Give the children a few minutes to plan out their sculptures.

- Then one at a time, invite each group to perform its "body sculpture."

- Have the other children try to guess which symbol is being scultped.

- Let every group have the opportunity to show its sculpture.

Symbols Worship Parade

Supplies: *Leaders' Guide—p. 39, signs and symbols made earlier, praise music CD, CD player*

Preparation:

- *Photocopy "My Family Helps Me Worship" (p. 39) for each child.*

- Have the children hold their "signs and symbols" paper plates and parade around the room as music plays.

- End the parade in front of your worship center. Have the children sit down.

- Call out the name of one of the symbols represented on the paper plates. Have the children who outlined that symbol stand.

Ask: What does this symbol mean?

- Encourage the children to tell you what the symbol means.

- Have the children sit back down.

- After the symbol is shared have all the children say: Symbols help us worship!

- Continue until you have named each symbol from the paper plates.

Symbol Praise Song

- Sing the following song with the children to tune of *"Three Blind Mice."*

Symbols here.
Symbols there.
See how they look.
See how they look.
They all remind us of God's great love.
They shower our lives with gifts from above.
You've never seen such a sight in your life
As symbols here.
Symbols there

Pray: Thank you, God, for worship symbols. They teach us about your love for us. They teach us about Jesus, our church, and our Bible. They teach us about our faith. Thank you for the many beautiful symbols in our church. We pray in Jesus' name. Amen.

- *Send home "My Family Helps Me Worship."*

Worship the Lord With Gladness: God's Children in Worship

 # My Family Helps Me Worship

Church Symbols Help Children Worship God

Your child learned about symbols in worship and their meaning. They viewed several worship symbols. We talked about ways worship symbols help us worship God.

Talk Points for the Week

Talk with your child about symbols. Name some symbols, such as the flag or a heart. Let your child tell you what the symbol stands for. Have your child share with you some of the symbols he or she learned about that are found in worship.

Family Worship

Set up a worship center in your home. Let the children in the family help select a place for the center and find items to place on your table.

How to Set Up Your Worship Center

1. Select a small table or card table.

2. Find a cloth to place on your table. You might wish to select a cloth that is the color of the liturgical season in the church.

3. Place some symbols of worship on your worship table. Some of the items you might select: Bible, cross, flowers, butterfly (symbol of resurrection), egg (new life), shell (symbol of baptism), dove (Holy Spirit), candles.

4. Invite your child to place his or her stained-glass butterfly on the worship table.

Worship God With Scripture

Place water in a large bowl. Gather twelve small stones. Read Joshua 4.

Tell the family the story of Joshua and the twelve stones at the Jordan River. This is the story your child learned in our worship session. Allow your child to help you tell the story.,

Read the Bible verse: Joshua 4:6: *"This will be a symbol among you. In the future your children may ask, 'What do these stones mean?'*

Let family members take turns dropping a stone into the bowl of water. As they drop each stone, have the family member dropping the stone into the water say: "What do these stones mean?"

The leader will respond to the question each time a stone is dropped.

What do these stones mean?

God is faithful.
God protects us.
God knows our names.
God gave us this family.
God is always with us.
God is kind.

God loves us.
God travels with us.
God helps us.
God is good.
God watches over us.

Our stones are symbols of God's care for us.

Worship Litany
Faith Symbols

Leader: The dove is the symbol for the Holy Spirit

Family: Come, Holy Spirit!

Leader: The Bible is God's Word.

Family: Thank you, God, for the Bible.

Leader: The cross reminds us of Jesus.

Family: Thank you, Jesus.

Leader: The butterfly reminds us that Jesus is alive!

Family: He is risen, alleluia!

Leader: We light a candle to provide light. God's love shines on our family.

Family: The love of God shines in the darkness.

Leader: The egg is a symbol of new life.

Family: Jesus makes our life beautiful!

Pray: Our family thanks you, God, for worship symbols that we find in our church sanctuary and here in our home. They remind us of your love for us. They help us worship you.

All: Thank you, God! Amen.

Worship the Lord With Gladness: God's Children in Worship

Music Helps Children Offer Praise

6

Bible Verses: Praise God with the blast of the ram's horn! Praise God with lute and lyre! Praise God with drum and dance! Praise God with strings and pipe! Praise God with loud cymbals! Praise God with clashing cymbals! Let every living thing praise the LORD! Praise the LORD! (*Psalm 150:3-6*)

Children will:

• Examine the Bible verses.

• Learn about musical instruments in the Bible.

• Identify musical instruments used today to worship God.

• Explore ways music helps children offer praise to God.

Worship Wisdom

The Book of Psalms is the hymnal and poetry book of the Jewish people. Some believe Psalm 150 was written after the Exile in Babylon (587-538 b.c.), a period of time in which the Jewish people were deported from their homeland. It was sung in the rebuilt Temple in Jerusalem as a way to offer thanksgiving to God.

Psalm 150 was used when large crowds of people gathered to worship together. Psalm 150:3-5 affirms that there are a variety of ways to praise God. We not only praise God with words, but we also strive to produce pleasant and beautiful sounds of music. A true offering of music, viewed as a gift from God, enhances our praise of God.

In Bible times, there were three groups of instruments: the ones you hit, such as drums and cymbals; the ones you blew into, such as horns and pipes; and the ones that had strings, such as harps. We discover that all of these instrument types are mentioned in Psalm 150:3-5. Note that before the psalmist even names each worship instrument, the writer captures the reader's attention with the passionate words, "Praise God."

The psalmist reminds the reader of the central function of worship music: to offer praise to God. With whatever instrument is used, the musician is instructed by the psalmist to praise God. Furthermore, the praise renderings of the musician should direct the listener's attention to God. The musician not only praises God through music, but leads and guides others to praise God, as well.

Today we praise God with a variety of musical forms and instruments. Some of our modern-day instruments are similar to instruments used in the Bible, yet some are unique to our times. Today we might use the organ, piano, guitar, drums, and keyboard as a part of our worship services. We can praise God with all types of instruments.

What is vitally important and absolutely necessary is that musicians offer their musical gifts to God with dignity, with enthusiasm, and with an attitude of sincere thanksgiving. Listeners should not only appreciate the gifts of the musician but also allow his or her musical offerings to enable them to truly worship God, just as the Psalms enabled the Jewish people to offer their own joyful praises.

 **Enter With Gladness**

As the Children Arrive

Supplies: *praise CD, CD player*

• Have some instrumental worship music playing as children arrive.

• Greet each child by name. As each child enters, express gladness that he or she is present.

The Music of the Bible

Supplies: Reproducible 9—p. 104, *pencils*

• *Photocopy "Praise God With. . ." (Reproducible 5) for each child.*

• Give each child "Praise God With…" and a pencil. Have the children use the code at the top of the page to fill in the missing spaces and learn the names of Bible instruments.

• Explain to the children about each instrument used in Bible times. An excellent Internet resource for Bible musical instruments is: info@MusicoftheBible.com. Click on "instruments."

Lyre: ancient type stringed instrument

Reed pipe: woodwind instrument with a nasal, piercing tone, similar to modern oboes and English horns, used for celebrations and funerals

Cymbals: similar to our cymbals used today, often used to give singers their pitch and to praise God in worship.

Shofar: hollow horn from an animal, often a ram, used to call the people to worship.

Lute: stringed instrument, similar to a guitar

View the Worship Center

Supplies: *small table, cloth, musical instruments, hymnal, choir anthems, musical notes, choir robes, hand bells*

Preparation:

• *Set up a worship center at a visible location in your room. Cover a small table with a cloth.*

• *Place some music items used in your worship service on the table.*

• Show the children the music items on your worship center.

Ask: What are some musical instruments we use in our worship service?

• As a child names an instrument, let the children respond, "Praise God!"

Ask: What are the names of some the choirs we have at our church?

• As a child names a choir, let the children respond, "Praise God!"

 Bible Praise Notes

Learn the Bible Verses

Supplies: *Bibles*

• Give each child a Bible. Show the children how to find the Book of Psalms in their Bible.

Say: Hold your Bible closed with the pages up and the spine down. Place your thumbs in the middle of the pages. Use your thumbs to open the Bible at the middle. You should be in or near the Book of Psalms.

• Show the children where Psalm 150 is found in the Book of Psalms.

• Let the children close their Bibles, find the Book of Psalms, and then find Psalm 150.

- Read Psalm 150:3-6 to the children.

Say: Bible people used many instruments to worship God. Today we use many instruments to worship God. Music helps us worship God.

- Divide the children into five groups: horn group, lute and lyre group, drum and dance group, strings and pipe group, and cymbals group. Show the children how to pretend they are playing a musical instrument in each group.

  Horn group—pretend to blow a horn

  Lute and lyre group—pretend to play a stringed instrument

  Drum and dance group—part of the group pretend to play the drums, and part of the group dance

  Strings and pipe—pretend to play a stringed instrument

  Cymbals—pretend to clang the cymbals together

- Read Psalm 150:3-5. When a group's instrument is named, have the children in that group pretend to play that instrument.

Play Musical Instruments

Supplies: *rhythm instruments*

- Give the children musical instruments. Let them remain in their musical instrument groups.

- Read Psalm 150:3-5. When a particular instrument group is named, have the children in that group play their musical instruments.

Musical Instruments Search

Supplies: Reproducible 10—p. 105, *pencils*

Preparation:

- *Photocopy "Musical Instrument Search" (Reproducible 10) for each child.*

- Give each child "Musical Instrument Search."

- Let the children find the words in the puzzle and circle the words. Assist nonreaders.

- Remind the children that these are the instruments mentioned in the Bible verses found in Psalm 150:3-5. Read the verses to the children again.

 # Let's Learn to Worship

Instrument Sounds

Supplies: *posterboard or large sheets of paper, marker, tape*

Preparation:

- *Display the posterboard or large paper on the wall or door where all the children can see it.*

- Encourage the children to think of musical instruments used in worship, both in Bible times and today. List each instrument named on the posterboard.

- Let the children work in pairs. Whisper to each pair a musical instrument from the list.

- Let the children have a few minutes to work in pairs to decide how that musical instrument

sounds when being played.

- Let the children, in pairs, practice making the sound of the musical instrument assigned to them.

- After a few minutes of practice time, have the children sit down on the floor with their partner.

Say: Psalm 150 tells us to praise God with different kinds of musical instruments. Listen carefully. I'm going to say, *"Praise God with the"* and then name a musical instrument. When you and your partner hear the name of the musical instrument assigned to you, jump up and make the sound of that instrument.

- Continue the game until you have named each pair's instrument.

Make a Musical Bell Instrument

Supplies: *elastic, yarn, small bells, small safety pins*

Preparation:

- *Cut a six-inch piece of elastic and a four-inch piece of yarn for each child.*

- Give each child four bells. Show the children how to slip the yarn through the bell loop and tie it to the elastic. Use small safety pins to fasten the two ends of the elastic together.

- Let the children place the bell instruments on their wrists. Have the children sing some praise songs as they ring their bells.

Invite Musicians

- Invite several musicians who play different musical instruments to visit your worship session.

- Have the musicians show the children how to play the instruments and tell the children how the instruments are used in worship.

- Invite the musicians to play their instruments.

Dance to Worship God

Supplies: *scarf or piece of fabric, praise CD, CD player, bells made earlier*

Say: Psalm 150 tells us not only to praise God with musical instruments, but also with dance.

- Give each child a scarf or piece of fabric. Put on a CD of praise music. Encourage the children to dance as they wave their scarves.

- Have the children wave their scarves to one side and then the other as they sway to the music.

- Have the children hold each end of their scarves and wave them above their heads as they sway.

- Let the children choose partners. Have each child tie one end of his or her scarf to the scarf of his or her partner. Have each child grab the other end of his or her scarf and move in pairs.

- Have each child tie his or her scarf to the bell instrument he or she made. Let each child put the bell instrument on his or her wrist.

- Have the children play their bell instruments with their scarves attached as they dance.

A Visit From Charles Wesley

Supplies: *hymnals*

- Invite a singer in your church who is familiar with the hymns of Charles Wesley. Let this individual play the role of Charles Wesley. Have her or him share with the children the following monologue:

How many of you like music? *(Pause for the response of the children.)* I do, too! I like music so much that I wrote over six thousand hymns for the people called Methodist. Some of you have probably heard of my brother John. He was the man who helped start the Methodist church. We lived in England. We were both preachers, and we worked together to help the Methodist people grow in their faith. Methodists have sung my hymns for over two hundred years. Today, many people use my hymns in their worship time.

- Have Charles Wesley hand out *United Methodist Hymnals* to the children.

- Have him call out several hymn numbers, one at a time. Instruct the actor to select only hymns written by Charles Wesley.

- Let the children find the hymn when he calls out a number. Let older children help the younger ones find the page with the hymn on it.

- Have Charles Wesley sing a verse of each hymn for the children.

Children Thank Worship Musicians

Supplies: *baby food jars, ribbon, candy, musical stickers*

- Let the children decorate the jars with musical stickers, including the lid.

- Have the children fill each baby food jar with candy, and then place the lid on each jar.

- Help the children tie a ribbon around each baby food jar.

- Invite them to present their gifts to musicians in your church.

We Worship God

Praise God with Musical Instruments and Singing Voices

Supplies: *rhythm instruments*

- Give the children the rhythm instruments.

- Have the children play their instruments as they sing some of their favorite praise songs or worship choruses.

Praise God With Scripture and Motion

Supplies: *Bible*

- Read Psalm 150:3-6 to the children. When you say the words, "Praise the Lord," have the children clap their hands.

- Read Psalm 150:3-6 to the children. When you mention a musical instrument in the Bible verses, have the children wave their hands in the air.

- Read Psalm 150:3-6 to the children. When you mention the word "dance" have the children start dancing, as you read the rest of the verse.

Watch and Worship

Supplies: *video of worship musical presentation, television or screen, the appropriate player*

Preparation:

- *Secure a video of a special worship musical presentation or choir cantata. Your church may have one, or you can borrow one from another church. Try to find a video that shows both singing and musical instruments.*

- Let the children watch and observe musical instruments used in the worship time. Have the children identify musical instruments. Let the children identify singers they may know.

- Discuss how the music helped the individuals who were listening to the music worship God.

Ask: How does the music in our worship service help you worship God?

- Identify children in your session who sing in the children's choir, play hand bells, or play a musical instrument.

- Thank the children for their service to your church. Affirm their gifts and remind them that children can offer music that praises God and helps others worship.

Sing a Worship Song

Supplies: *Leaders' Guide—p. 45*

Preparation:

- *Photocopy "My Family Helps Me Worship" (p. 45) for each child.*

- Sing the song printed below with the children. The song is sung to the tune of "Praise God, Praise God, All Ye Little Children."

Praise God, praise God, with the sound of organ.
Worship God. Worship God.
Praise God, praise God, with the sound of organ.
Worship God. Worship God.

- Add other verses:

Praise God, praise God, with the grand piano.
Praise God, praise God, with the drums and cymbals.
Praise God, praise God, with guitars a'strumming.
Praise God, praise God, with the bells a'ringing.
Praise God, praise God, with the voice of singing.
Praise God, praise God, with the feet of dancing.
Praise God, praise God, with the sound of music.

Pray: Thank you, God, for music. Thank you for our musicians who use their talents to help us worship God. We'll lift our singing voices in praise to you. We'll dance to music to offer our thanks. We'll listen joyfully to instruments that make beautiful sounds, and we'll gladly hear singing voices that lead us to worship our God. We pray in the name of Jesus. Amen.

- Send *"My Family Helps Me Worship"* home with each child.

My Family Helps Me Worship

Music Helps Children Offer Praise

Your child learned that music helps him or her worship God. We used the words from Psalm 150:3-6 to teach your child about the variety of instruments used in Bible times.

Talk Points for the Week

Ask: What are some of the musical instruments that were used in Bible times to praise God?

Ask: What's your favorite musical instrument used in our worship service at church?

Say: Tell me about Charles Wesley.

Sing some of your child's favorite worship songs.

Put on some worship music and dance with your child.

Look for musical instruments while watching television. Let your child share with you if he or she has seen a particular instrument used in our worship service.

Family Worship

Set up a worship center in your home. Let the children in the family help you select a place for your worship center and items to place on your worship table.

How to Set Up Your Worship Center

1. Select a small table or card table.
2. Find a cloth to place on your center. Cover the worship center with the cloth. You might wish to select a cloth that is the color of the liturgical season in the church.
3. Place some sheet music, musical instruments, and music notes on your worship table. Place other items in your worship center that reminds your family of music.

Worship God With Scripture

Read Psalm 150:3-6

When you say the words "Praise God," have family members lift their hands in praise.

When you read a musical instrument, have family members pretend to play a musical instrument.

When you use the word cymbals, have family members pretend to clang cymbals together.

Praise God With Dance

Play a CD of praise music. Have family members join hands. Have them make a dancing motion as they move to the right, to the left, toward the inside of your circle, and toward the outside of your circle. Repeat several times. End by letting go of each other's hands and shouting, "Praise God!"

Worship God With Instruments

Let family members who sing or play musical instruments share a song or instrumental piece for family members. As you listen, worship God, and give thanks for the gifts of family members.

Family Sing-along

If a member of your family plays the piano, gather around and sing some favorite praise choruses or hymns. Or sing them a cappella if you do not have any musical instruments available to accompany the family singing.

YouTube Praise

Gather the family around the computer. Get on YouTube. Select some of your favorite Christian artists. Listen to some of their songs. Use this as a time of worship.

One Service, Many Parts

7

Bible Verse: For where two or three are gathered in my name, I'm there with them. *(Matthew 18:20)*

Children will:

- Examine the Bible verse.
- Explore the various parts of the worship service.
- Learn about the Lord's Prayer and the Apostles' Creed.
- Understand the parts of the worship bulletin.

Worship Wisdom

This particular verse of Scripture has often been isolated from its context in the Gospel of Matthew. Most often it is quoted to speak of Christ's presence in the midst of worship. A close examination of the Scripture reveals to us that Matthew is primarily speaking of a situation in the church in which individuals demonstrate conflict toward one another. Matthew seeks to resolve the conflict and instruct the community of faith on how to bring the bickering parties back into harmony with one another.

Jesus wants us to know that when we seek reconciliation with one another in the body of Christ, he is present. Jesus breaks down all barriers that divide us as brothers and sisters in Christ and as children of God.

However, understanding this interpretation does not mean that we cannot use this verse of Scripture to talk with our children about the presence of Christ in our worship service, in the gatherings for Christian fellowship, and in our expressions of family life. Christ is always with us. It is impossible to have Christian fellowship by ourselves; rather, we need each other. And it only takes two or three Christians in harmony with one another for Christian fellowship to become a reality.

In the Jewish tradition, ten males were required to form a synagogue. Matthew was well aware of this tradition, as he was Jewish. Matthew indicates to us that in the assembling of believers in Christ, Jesus does not limit his presence to a large gathering of God's people. Rather, he abides with his followers, even if there are only a few of the faithful gathered together.

In our modern society, we have a tendency to place value on large numbers. Matthew reminds us that Jesus does not judge an individual church by the number of persons that show up nor does Christ exclusively limit his presence to the congregation of a mega-church. Rather, Jesus dwells in the midst of those who seek to worship him, regardless of whether there is a huge crowd of worshipers or a dedicated handful of believers.

46

 **Enter With Gladness**

As the Children Arrive

Supplies: *paper, crayons or markers*

- Greet each child by name. As each child enters, express gladness that he or she is present.

- Give each child a piece of paper and let the child draw his or her favorite part of worship.

- Encourage the children share their drawings.

Say: There are many parts to our worship service. We'll learn about some of these parts today.

Visit the Worship Center

Supplies: *Reproducibles 13-14—pp. 108-109, Bible, hymnal, bulletin, offering plate, praying hands, copy of the Lord's Prayer or praying hands, copy of the Apostles' Creed, children's worship bag, item to represent Children's Worship or Children's Sermon time, attendance pads, pencils, drawings made earlier*

Preparation:

- *Photocopy the "Apostles' Creed" (Reproducible 13) and "The Lord's Prayer" (Reproducible 14).*

- *Set up a worship center on a small table. Cover the table with a cloth.*

- *Place on the table some items used in your worship service that represent parts of your service.*

- Gather the children around the worship center. As you hold up an item in your worship center, let the children tell you where in your worship service, they might see that item being used.

Note: Not every church will have these parts, so select the parts of the worship service that are used in your worship service.

Bible—Part of the service where we read the Scripture.

Hymnal—Part of the service where we sing.

Offering plate—Part of the service where we give our money.

Item for Children's Sermon—Part of the service when children come forward and hear a story or lesson about God and Jesus.

Item for Children's Worship—Part of the service when children leave the sanctuary for their own special worship time.

Praying Hands—Part of the service when we pray. We say the Lord's Prayer together.

Apostles' Creed—Words we say together as a congregation that teach us about the birth, death, and resurrection of Jesus.

- Let the children place their drawings of their favorite parts of worship on the worship table. Have the children shake hands with one another.

Say: Another part of some worship services is the time of greeting one another. We call this "Passing the Peace of Christ." During this time, persons show their love for one another. This is a happy time in the worship service.

- Encourage the children to participate in the *Passing the Peace of Christ*, Greeting Time, or whatever you call it in your church, if that is a part of the tradition in your church. If not, encourage the children to greet persons before or after the worship service.

- If you use attendance pads in your congregation, encourage children to feel welcome to sign their names to the attendance pads.

Bible Praise Notes

Learn the Bible Verse

Supplies: *Bible, construction paper, tape*

- Show the children where Matthew 18:20 is found in the Bible. Read the verse to them.

Ask: How many people must be present in church for Jesus to be present with them? *(2 or 3)*

- Encourage the children make megaphones.

- Give each child a piece of construction paper. Show the children how to roll the paper into a cone. Help the children tape the edges together.

- Divide the children into two groups. Let group one shout into their megaphones, "For where two or three are gathered in my name."

- Have group two shout into their megaphones, "I'm there with them."

- Reverse and let group two shout into their megaphones, "For where two or three are gathered in my name."

- Have group one shout into their megaphones, "I'm there with them."

- Have the children use their megaphones and shout the entire Bible verse together as a group.

- Have the children use their megaphones and whisper the Bible verse together as a group.

- Have the children use their megaphones and start saying the Bible verse softly, and then increase in volume.

- Have the children use their megaphones and say the Bible verse to other children.

- Have the children shout the Bible verse into their megaphones, pointing their megaphones to the left, to the right, in the air, and downward.

Reinforce the Bible Verse

Supplies: Bible, Reproducible 11—p. 106, *scissors, tape*

Preparation:

- *Photocopy "Bible Verse Chain" (Reproducible 11) for each child.*

- Give each child "Bible Verse Chain." Have the children cut out the word strips.

- Read Matthew 18:20 to the children. Have the children to put their word strips in order.

- Encourage each child to make a chain with their word strips. Begin with the word strip, "For where." Have the children form a circle with the strip by taping the ends together.

- Next take the strip "two or three." Loop the strip through the "For where" strip and tape the ends together. Continue until each child has a complete Bible verse chain.

Two or Three

- Teach the children the song "Two or Three" to the tune of "This Old Man."

Two or Three

Two or three, two or three,
(Have children hold up two fingers and then three.)

All it takes is you and me.
(Have children point to other children.)

With a person here and a person there,
(Have children move left hand and then right hand in a sweeping motion.)

We feel God's presence everywhere.
(Bring both hands inward and place on heart.)

 **Let's Learn to Worship**

One Service, Many Parts

Supplies: Reproducible 12—p. 107, *pencils*

Preparation:

- *Photocopy "Worship Words" (Reproducible 12) for each child.*

- Give each child "Worship Words." Let each child draw a line from the worship word to the picture that goes along with it.

- Help younger children or have them work in pairs with an older child.

- Go over each word and talk with the children about the definition.

Ask: When have you seen people putting these words into action in worship?

Blooming Flowers of Worship

Supplies: Reproducible 12—p. 107, *paper plates, cupcake papers, craft sticks, markers, glue, tape, scissors, stapler and staples, yarn, paper punch*

Preparation:

- *Photocopy "Worship Words" (Reproducible 12) for each child.*

- *Cut paper plates in half. Each child will need one whole plate and one half plate.*

- Give each child a whole paper plate and a half paper plate.

Say: We're going to make a worship word garden. First we need to make the garden.

- Let the children decorate their paper plates to be a garden. They might color the half paper plate green. They might color the top half of the whole paper plate blue and the bottom half green. They could even add clouds and birds.

- Help each child staple the half paper plate to the bottom of the whole paper plate to make a pocket.

- Punch a hole in the top of the whole paper plate. Help each child tie a length of yarn through the hole to make a hanger.

- Give the children "Worship Words" and seven craft sticks.

- Have each child cut out the picture circles and the words.

- Give each child an envelope. Show the children how to cut off the flap of the envelope.

- Have the children glue the envelope front-side down on the pocket of their gardens.

- Have the children place their seven words in the envelope pockets.

- Give each child seven cupcake papers. Show the child how to glue a worship picture in the center of each cupcake paper to make flowers.

- Have the child glue each flower to a craft stick.

- Let the children place their seven flowers inside the paper plate pocket.

- Have the children draw a worship word out of the envelope, and then pull out the flower that matches the word.

- Encourage the children to take their craft project home and use with their families.

Worship Bulletins

Supplies: *Bible stickers, smiley face stickers, praying hand stickers, cross stickers, music note stickers, worship bulletins*

- Give each child a copy of your worship bulletin, one or two Bible stickers, one smiley face sticker, one praying hand sticker, one cross sticker, and two or three music note stickers.

- Have the children look at their worship bulletins. Show them where in the service the Bible is read. Have each child place a Bible sticker by the Scripture reading or readings.

- Show the children where in the service a prayer takes place. Have each child place a praying hands sticker by the prayer time.

- Show the children where in the service there is a hymn or choir anthem. Have each child place music note stickers by the hymns and other musical presentations.

- Show the children where in the service the sermon occurs. Have each child place a cross sticker by the sermon time.

- Show the children where in the service the children's sermon takes place or where in the service children leave the sanctuary for children's worship. Have each child place a smiley sticker where that time occurs in your worship service.

The Lord's Prayer

Supplies: Reproducible 14—p. 109

Say: The disciples asked Jesus to teach them how to pray. Jesus responded by teaching his disciples the Lord's Prayer. We say the Lord's Prayer in our worship service, and we remember that this is a special prayer because the words of the prayer came from Jesus.

- Repeat the prayer for the children. Let the children say the prayer along with you, as much as they know of it. Encourage the children to memorize the Lord's Prayer.

- Teach the children motions to use with the Lord's Prayer:

Our Father, who art in heaven,
(raise hands upward toward heaven)

hallowed be thy name.
(place hands in a prayer motion)

Thy kingdom come, thy will be done
(stretch hands outward)

on earth as it is in heaven.
(point finger upward)

Give us this day our daily bread.
(clasp hands together)

And forgive us our trespasses,

as we forgive those who trespass against us.
(place hands on heart)

And lead us not into temptation,
    but deliver us from evil.
(clasp hands together and release quickly)

For thine is the kingdom, and the power,
    and the glory, forever.
(move hands to the left, right, and center)

Amen.
(everyone say together)

From the Ritual of the Former Methodist Church

The Apostles' Creed

Supplies: Reproducible 13—p. 108, *scissors, posterboard, markers*

Preparation:

- *Photocopy the "Apostles' Creed "(Reproducible 13). Cut out the sections and glue them on six pieces of posterboard. Leave space for the children to draw on each of the six pieces of posterboard.*

Section One: I believe in God the Father Almighty, maker of heaven and earth;

Section Two: And in Jesus Christ his only Son, our Lord:

Section Three: who was conceived by the Holy Spirit, born of the Virgin Mary, suffered under Pontius Pilate, was crucified, dead, and buried;

Section Four: the third day he rose from the dead;

Section Five: he ascended into heaven, and sitteth at the right hand of God the Father Almighty; from thence he shall come to judge the quick and the dead.

Section Six: I believe in the Holy Spirit, the holy catholic church, the communion of saints, the forgiveness of sins, the resurrection of the body, and the life everlasting. Amen.

The Apostles' Creed, Traditional Version

- Read the Apostles' Creed to the children. Briefly explain it as you read each section.

Say: In worship services, worshipers sometimes say creeds. Creeds tell us what we believe. One of the best known of our creeds is the Apostles' Creed. Christians have said the creed for thousands of years. This creed tells us what we believe about God, Jesus, the Holy Spirit, and our faith.

Say: (Section One) God is our Creator. God made everything good.

(Section Two) We believe in Jesus, God's Son.

(Section Three) We believe that Jesus was born to a woman named Mary. Pontius Pilate was one of the chief leaders at the time Jesus was put to death. We believe Jesus died and was buried in a tomb.

(Section Four) God raised Jesus from the dead. Jesus is alive! We celebrate his resurrection on Easter Sunday.

(Section Five) Jesus now lives with God in heaven. One day he will return to earth.

(Section Six) We believe in the Holy Spirit. The church is a group of believers who can

be found all over the world. We believe God forgives our sins and that when we die, we will live forever with God.

- Divide the children into six groups. Give each group the posterboard for one section of The Apostles' Creed.

- Let the groups decide what to draw on their posterboard. Encourage them to think of something that helps them understand that part of the Apostle's Creed.

- Display their artwork during the Let's Worship God time.

Praising God Through the Doxology

Supplies: hymnal

Say: One of the ways many churches praise God in their worship services is through the singing of the Doxology.

- Teach the doxology (The United Methodist Hymnal, 95) to the children. Let them sing it several times.

- If your church uses a different song with the presentation of the offering, teach the song to the children at this time.

 # We Worship God

Share in a Call to Worship

- Let the children share in a call to worship.

Say: The call to worship is a part of the worship service that is used at the beginning to invite us to worship God.

- Say the following call to worship, "One Service, Many Parts," with the children.

- Have the children respond with the words: "One service, many parts."

One Service, Many Parts

Leader: Jesus said, "Where two or three are gathered for worship. I am there."

Children: One service, many parts.

Leader: Jesus is present when we share our call to worship and read Scripture.

Children: One service, many parts.

Leader: Jesus is present when we sing a hymn or listen to the choir.

Children: One service, many parts.

Leader: Jesus is present when we pray or listen to a sermon.

Children: One service, many parts.

Leader: Jesus is present when we give our offering or share "The Peace of Christ."

Children: One service, many parts.

The Lord's Prayer

- Invite the children to close their eyes and listen as you say the Lord's Prayer.

- Say the prayer again and let the children do the motions to the Lord's Prayer they learned in the worship section (p. 50).

- Have the children say the Lord's Prayer together. Assure the children that you understand some have not memorized the prayer. Let them say as many words as they can.

Share the Peace of Christ

- Divide the children into pairs. Have the children practice "Passing the Peace of Christ."

- Have one child say to the other child, "The peace of Christ be with you." Have the other child respond, "And also with you."

- Have the children walk around the room and greet one another.

The Apostles' Creed

Supplies: *The Apostles' Creed artwork made earlier.*

- Display the artwork on the Apostles' Creed for all the children to view.

- After you read each section of the Apostles' Creed, let the children explain their art.

Sing to God

- Let the children sing some songs or hymns.

Respect the Bible

Supplies: *Bible*

- Have the children sit in a circle on the floor or a rug. Hand the Bible to a child. Show the child how to lift up the Bible as a sign of respect.

- After the child does this, have him or her pass the Bible to the next child. Encourage the children to continue passing the Bible around the circle and lifting it up until all the children have participated.

Offer a Benediction of Blessing

Supplies: Leaders' Guide—pp. 53-54

Preparation:

- *Photocopy "My Family Helps Me Worship" (p. 53) and "Prayers and Creeds" (p. 54) for each child.*

- Go around the circle and place your hands gently on the head of each child as you share the benediction from Numbers 6:24-26. Repeat the blessing as many times as needed.

Say: The benediction is said at the end of a worship service. It's often a blessing that helps us remember to serve God during the week.

The Lord bless you and keep you.
The Lord make his face shine on you,
*   and be gracious to you.*
The Lord lift up his face to you,
*   and grant you peace.*

Say: Thank you, God, that Jesus is present with us whenever we gather for worship whether there are a few people or lots of people. Thank you for the many parts of our worship service that help us praise and serve God. Thank you for prayers and creeds that help us learn about Jesus and our faith. We pray in Jesus' name. Amen.

- Send *"My Family Helps Me Worship"* and *"Prayers and Creeds"* home with each child.

My Family Helps Me Worship

One Service, Many Parts

Your child learned about the many parts of our worship service that help us praise God.

Talk Points for the Week

Ask: What are some of your favorite parts of the worship service?

Pray the Lord's Prayer together. Encourage your child to memorize the Lord's Prayer.

Family Worship

Set up a worship center in your home. Let the children in the family help you select a place for your worship center and items to place on your worship table.

How to Set Up Your Worship Center

1. Select a small table or card table.

2. Find a cloth to place on your center. Cover the table with the cloth. You might wish to select a cloth that is the color of the liturgical season.

3. Place symbols of worship on your worship table that represent the parts of our church worship service such as a hymnal (singing), a Bible (preaching and reading Scripture), a basket with play money inside (offering), and a bulletin.

Worship God with Scripture

Read Matthew 18:20.

Ask family members to take turns naming places they go during the week. When a family members names a place, have the other family members respond with the words "Jesus is with you."

One Service, Many Parts

Give each family member a party blower.

Name an item on your worship table and share with family members the part of our worship service that the item represents. When you name a part of our worship service, have family members blow their party blowers as a way of giving thanks for that part of the worship service.

Sing

Sing the African song, "Kum Ba Ya" printed in "Prayers and Creeds."

The Doxology and Offering

Ask family members to write down on a small piece of paper what he or she could offer God during the week.

Have family members place their papers in the basket on your worship table and sing "The Doxology" (printed in "Prayers and Creeds").

The Lord's Prayer

Teach family members the motions to "The Lord's Prayer" printed in "Prayers and Creeds." Let your child assist. Say the Lord's Prayer as a family, using the motions.

The Apostles' Creed

Read the Apostles' Creed printed in "Prayers and Creeds" to the family. Let family members blow their party blowers after you read each section of the creed.

Benediction

Bless family members with the benediction printed in "Prayers and Creeds." Lift one hand upward to bless family members or use similar motions your pastor uses when he or she offers a benediction.

Pray: Thank you, God, for our family worship time and our church worship time. Thank you for the many parts of our church worship service. Thank you for Jesus who is with us when we worship and wherever we go. Amen.

Prayers and Creeds

Kum Ba Yah

Sing the first verse, and then repeat the song using the following words to remind your family of the various parts of our worship service:

Kum ba yah, my Lord, kum ba yah.
Kum ba yah, my Lord, kum ba yah.
Kum ba yah, my Lord, kum ba yah.
O Lord, kum ba yah!

Afro-American spiritual

Someone's praying, Lord
Someone's singing, Lord
Someone's preaching, Lord
Someone's reading, Lord
Someone's giving, Lord
Someone's greeting, Lord

The Doxology

Praise God, from whom all blessings flow;
praise him, all creatures here below;
praise him above, ye heavenly host;
praise Father, Son, and Holy Ghost. Amen.

The Lord's Prayer

Our Father, who art in heaven,
(raise hands upward toward heaven)

hallowed be thy name.
(place hands in a prayer motion)

Thy kingdom come, thy will be done
(stretch hands outward)

on earth as it is in heaven.
(point finger upward)

Give us this day our daily bread.
(clasp hands together)

And forgive us our trespasses,
   as we forgive those who trespass against
   us.
(place hands on heart)

And lead us not into temptation,
   but deliver us from evil
(clasp hands together and release quickly)

For thine is the kingdom, and the power,
   and the glory, forever.
(move hands to the left, right, and center)

Amen. *(everyone say together)*

From the Ritual of the Former Methodist Church

The Apostles' Creed

I believe in God the Father Almighty,
maker of heaven and earth; *(blow party horns)*

And in Jesus Christ his only Son our Lord:
  who was conceived by the Holy Spirit,
    born of the Virgin Mary,
    suffered under Pontius Pilate,
    was crucified, dead and buried; *(blow party horns)*

the third day he rose from the dead;
he ascended into heaven,
  and sitteth at the right hand of God the Father
    Almighty;
from thence he shall come to judge the quick and
    the dead. *(blow party horns)*

I believe in the Holy Spirit,
  the holy catholic church,
  the communion of saints,
  the forgiveness of sins,
  the resurrection of the body,
  and the life everlasting. *(blow party horns)*

Amen. *(blow party horns several times)*

The Apostles' Creed, Traditional Version

Benediction

*"The LORD bless you and keep you.
The LORD make his face shine on you,
  and be gracious to you.
The LORD lift up his face to you,
  and grant you peace." (Numbers 6:24-26)*

Worship the Lord With Gladness: God's Children in Worship

8 One God, Many Ways to Worship

Bible Verse: Come, let's worship and bow down!
Let's kneel before the LORD, our maker! *(Psalm 95:6)*

Children will:

• Examine the Bible verse.

• Explore ways to use movement in worship.

• Learn about ways to pray.

• Practice using their senses in worship.

 # Worship Wisdom

The Psalms are filled with suggestions on how to worship God. Although many of the Psalms are attributed to David, we are not sure who wrote all of them. Many of our Psalms were written as hymns of praise. They were to be sung by the people as they entered worship, as they engaged in worship, or as they left worship to live out their faith in the community.

Psalm 95 belongs to a group of psalms that celebrates the kingship of God. The psalmist declares that Yahweh reigns and that Yahweh is King. King David brought the ark of the covenant to Jerusalem and placed it in a special tent. The Ark, in this holy location, represented for the people the royalty or kingship of God. The ark of the covenant, which symbolized the very presence of God, also reminded the people of God's throne. The Jewish worshipers sang Psalm 95 as a psalm of praise, directed to King Yahweh, who sat on the royal throne, ruling in power and might.

Psalm 95 demands that worshipers engage in active worship. Bowing and kneeling are both acts of submission carried out in the presence of a person deemed worthy of honor. In Psalm 95, the writer declares that God is worthy of our worship

and deserves our acts of submission and humility. Bowing and kneeling are active, rather than passive acts of worship.

The children you teach are active worshipers. Children worship best when they are allowed to use all of their senses. They want to taste the Communion bread, they yearn to reach out and touch the pastor's stole, they enjoy smelling the altar flowers, they rejoice to hear the choir's anthems, and they are compelled to stare at the stained-glass windows. They rarely experience worship through passively sitting and observing, more likely their worship experience comes through actively engaging their senses in learning.

Worship can become an enriching, positive, and life-changing experience for children when congregations provide opportunities for children to use their God-created bodies and their God-gifted senses to praise God. Psalm 95 affirms inspired movement and enhanced sensory experiences in worship, and so must we!

 # Enter With Gladness

As the Children Arrive

• Greet each child by name. As each child enters, express gladness that he or she is present.

We Use Dance to Worship God

Supplies: *liturgical dancers, praise CD, CD player*

• Invite a liturgical dancer or dancers to be share a liturgical dance with the children.

• Let the children watch the dancing as they arrive.

Say: Our dancers are praising and worshiping God as they dance to the music.

Children Dance

Supplies: *Bible, strips of cloth or streamers, dowel sticks, tape, liturgical dancers, praise CD, CD player*

Preparation:

• Tape a strip of cloth or a length of streamer to a dowel stick for each child. Refer to these as praise sticks.

• Read Psalm 149:3a to the children: *"Let them praise God's name with dance."*

Say: One of the ways people worshiped God in the Bible was to dance. We can also worship through dance.

• Let the liturgical dancer or dancers show the children some simple dance steps.

• Have them dance using their praise sticks to move to the music and to dance.

View the Worship Center

Supplies: *Bible, paraments, flowers, bread, pastor's stole, candles, ballet or tap shoes*

Preparation:

• *Set up a worship center on a small table. Cover the table with a cloth.*

• *Borrow one of the worship paraments used in your church to cover your worship center. (Paraments are cloths placed on the pulpit, lectern, and Communion table to identify the church season.)*

• *Place items on your worship table that represent the use of the senses in worship. Some ideas are: flowers—sense of smell or sight; bread— sense of taste; pastor's stole—sense of touch; candles— sense of sight; ballet or tap shoes— worshiping God through dance; handprints— worshiping God by clapping.*

• Show the children the items on your worship center. Let the children use their senses to smell the flowers, touch the pastor's stole, taste some of the bread, and view the candles and other items.

• Read Psalm 47:1 to the children: *"Clap your hands, all you people! Shout joyfully to God with a joyous shout!"*

• Have the children clap their hands to worship God.

• Encourage the children to shout "Praise God!" as they leave the worship center.

Worship the Lord With Gladness: God's Children in Worship

 **Bible Praise Notes**

Learn the Bible Verse

Supplies: *Bible, Reproducible 15—p. 110*

Preparation:

* *Photocopy "Psalm 95:6" (Reproducible 15) for each child.*

* Read Psalm 95:6.

* Let the children repeat the verse several times.

* Learn the Bible Verse in sign language. Use "Psalm 95:6" to teach the children sign language for the Bible verse.

* Have the children practice signing the verse with a partner.

* Let the children sign the verse as a group as they say the verse together.

Bible Verse Motions

* Divide the children into two groups. Have them form two lines facing each other. Have one group say, "Come, let's worship and bow down! The group saying these words then bows.

* Let the other group say, "Let's kneel before the Lord, our maker!" Let that group kneel. Then reverse what each group says and reverse the motions each group does.

* Let all the children say the Bible verse and use the motions of bowing and kneeling.

Say: Bowing and kneeling are ways to show respect and honor to God.

* Have the children respond with the words, "The Lord, our maker" when you ask the following questions:

Who do we worship? (The Lord, our maker.)

Who do we bow down to? (The Lord, our maker.)

Who do we kneel before? (The Lord, our maker.)

Say: The word *Lord* is another word for God. God made you and all creation.

 # Let's Learn to Worship

Worship Word Search

Supplies: *Bible, Reproducible 16—p. 111, pencils*

Preparation:

* *Photocopy "Worship Word Search" (Reproducible 16) for each child.*

* Give each child "Worship Word Search." Let the older children find the words. Help the younger children find the words.

Say: These words tell us about different ways to worship God. Let the children repeat Psalm 95:6 using each of the motions:

Clap while saying the Bible verse.

Dance while saying the Bible verse.

Kneel while saying the Bible verse.

Shout while saying the Bible verse.

Bow while saying the Bible verse.

Lift hands in praise while saying the Bible verse.

Learn About Paraments

Supplies: *dry erase board and dry erase markers or a large sheet of paper, markers, and tape, optional: paraments*

Preparation:

- *Write the word* parament *on a dry erase board or large sheet of paper.*

Say: Paraments are special cloths that are placed on the pulpit, the lectern, and our Communion table to tell us the seasons of the church year.

- Take the children into your sanctuary and show them where the pulpit, lectern, and Communion table are located.

- If you are unable to tour the sanctuary, borrow some paraments used in your worship service and show them to the children.

Parts of Prayer

Say: In our worship service we use prayer as a way to talk to God.

- Teach the children what each part of prayer means.

Say: *Praise* means saying, "God, you are great and we love and worship you."

Thanks means saying, "Thank you, God."

Confession means saying, "God, I am sorry. Please forgive me."

Forgiveness means God saying to us, "I forgive you. I love you."

Petition means saying, "God, please help me."

Intercession means saying, "God, please be with my mother (or anyone you are praying for)".

- Read out the sentence prayers below. Let the children guess which type of prayer you are reading.

God, you are great, and we love and worship you. Thank you for being our Creator. *(Praise)*

Thank you, God, for my family. *(Thanks)*

God, I am sorry for yelling at my brother. Please forgive me. *(Confession)*

God, please help me remember the words to the speech I have to give in class. *(Petition)*

God, my grandmother is very sick. Please help her. *(Intercession)*

Parts of Prayer Game

Supplies: *large piece of plastic foam board, paint stirrers, paper plates, markers, tape*

Preparation:

- *Write each of the parts of prayer (Praise, Thanks, Confession, Forgiveness, Petition, Intercession) on a separate paper plate. Tape a paint stirrer to each plate to make a sign.*

- *Place the plastic foam board on a table.*

- Review the parts of prayer.

- Place the signs face-down on the table.

- Read out the meaning for a part of prayer.

- Select one child to go to the table and turn over only one of the signs. If he or she turns over the sign that matches the meaning of the part of prayer, he or she gets to stick that sign in the plastic foam board.

- If he or she does not get the correct match, he or she must turn the sign back face-down.

- Have that child select another child to play.

- Keep playing until all the signs with the words for parts of prayer have been matched with their meanings and placed in the plastic foam board.

- If time allows, you can reverse the game by reading out the meaning and having a child come forward and take the sign out of the plastic foam board and place it face-down on the table.

Jesus Says Game

- Play a game is like the game "Simon Says." The difference is that the leader uses the words, "Jesus says," rather than "Simon says," as you instruct the children to do certain worship motions.

Say: Let's play a game like "Simon Says." Do the motion I call out only if I say, "Jesus says." If I do not say, "Jesus says," before I call out a motion, stand still. If you move, you're out.

- Use the following motions: dance, bow, kneel, praise, clap and shout.

- Keep playing the game until only one child is left or the children tire of the game.

 # We Worship God

Worship Dance Parade

Supplies: *praise sticks, praise CD, CD player*

- Give the children their praise sticks to wave.

- Place the children in a line, with space between each child. Let them march around the room as they wave their praise sticks.

- Let them stand in a circle, with some distance between each child, and dance to praise music as they wave their praise sticks.

- Let the children imitate you as they wave their praise sticks in front, to the left, to the right, above their heads, and down toward the floor.

Bow-Kneel-Clap

- Start out saying very slowly the words *bow, kneel,* and *clap.*

- Let the children make the motion when you say the words.

- Gradually increase your speed as you say the words and the children do the motions.

Worship God with Song and Movement

Supplies: The United Methodist Hymnal, *singer or CD of* The United Methodist Hymnal, *CD player*

- Invite a singer to come and sing some hymns from The United Methodist Hymnal for the children. Suggest the individual sing hymns that remind the children of ways to worship God using movement.

Suggested Hymns:

No. 177—"He is Lord" (*Have the children bow and kneel.*)

No. 333—"I'm Goin' a Sing When the Spirit Says Sing" (*Have the singer substitute the word "sing" with the words "dance," "bow," "clap," "praise," "shout," and "kneel." When a particular motion is sung, have the children do that motion.*)

Prayers of Intercession

Supplies: Leaders' Guide—p. 60

Preparation:

- *Photocopy "My Family Helps Me Worship" (p. 60) for each child.*

Ask: Who do you know that needs our prayers?

- Let the children call out names.

- Say a prayer of intercession for persons the children name.

Pray: Thank you, God, for worship. We're glad that we can worship you in many ways. We can bow down, clap our hands, shout our praises, dance with joy, and kneel humbly before our God. Thank you for prayer and the parts of prayer we've learned about. We're glad you hear our prayers. We pray in Jesus' name. Amen.

Have children respond: Amen. So be it!

 # My Family Helps Me Worship

One God, Many Ways to Worship

Your child learned that we serve one God, but we may worship God in many ways. We can bow down to God to show honor and respect. We can clap our hands or dance to offer adoration. We can lift our hands in praise. We can kneel humbly before God when we pray. All of these ways of worshiping God are found in Scripture.

Your child also learned about different types of prayers. Just as there are many ways to worship God, there are also many forms of prayer.

Talk Points for the Week

Say: Show me how you bow, kneel, shout, dance, clap, and praise to worship God.

Share prayers throughout the week with your child.

Family Worship

Set up a worship center in your home. Let the children in the family help you select a place for your worship center and items to place on your worship table.

How to Set Up Your Worship Center

1. Select a small table or card table.

2. Find a cloth to place on your center. Cover the table with the cloth. You might wish to select a cloth that is the color of the liturgical season.

3. Place some items on your worship center that will help family members use their senses. Suggestions are: bread to taste, pleasant smelling flowers, fabric pieces to touch, a beautiful picture or item to view.

Worship God With Scripture

• Read Psalm 95:6.

• Repeat the Bible verse and have the family members do a different motion each time (clap, dance, kneel, shout, bow, lift hands in praise).

Praying Together

Offer sentence prayers that offer praise to God. (Praise means saying, "God, you are great and we love and worship you.")

Offer sentence prayers that thank God. (Thanks means saying, "Thank you, God.")

Offer sentence prayers of confession. (Confession means saying, "God, I am sorry. Please forgive me.")

Offer sentence prayers of petition. (Petition means saying, "God, please help me.")

Offer sentence prayers of intercession. (Intercession means saying, "God, please be with my grandfather [or anyone].")

Share a Worship Litany—Senses in Motion

Leader: God gave us the sense of smell. Bow down to God in praise!

(Have family members bow down to God.)

Leader: God gave us the sense of hearing. Clap your hands in praise!

(Have family members clap their hands.)

Leader: God gave us the sense of seeing. Kneel before God your Creator!

(Have family members kneel before God.)

Leader: God gave us the sense of touch. Let's dance before God.

(Have family members grab the hands of another family member and dance.)

Leader: God gave us the ability to shout our praises!

(Have family members shout: Praise the Lord!)

Pray: Thank you, God, for our bodies. Thank you for the gifts of smell, touch, sight, and sound. Thank you for hearing our prayers. We ask our prayer in the name of Jesus. Amen.

9 We Worship and We Welcome

Bible Verse: So welcome each other, in the same way that Christ also welcomed you, for God's glory. (*Romans 15:7*)

Children will:

- Examine the Bible verse.
- Explore the meaning of Christian hospitality.
- Learn ways they can express welcome and hospitality to others.
- Put into practice the concept of hospitality in worship.

 # Worship Wisdom

At the time Paul wrote his Letter to the Romans, Rome was one of the most important and powerful cities in the world. Rome boasted a vast army that controlled all of the countries that surrounded the Mediterranean Sea. In addition, Rome was a vital city for trade. The rulers of Rome were extremely wealthy and had many slaves. Against this background of power, exploitation, and greed, Paul advises the Christian believers to extend hospitality, even if this endeavor might appear at times to be a daunting and challenging task.

Paul had not visited Rome at the time he wrote his letter. Paul probably wrote this letter about A.D. 57. Paul wrote most of his letters to churches that he himself had established. The church at Rome was different, however. The church at Rome was already established. There were many worshiping Christians in Rome at the time Paul wrote his appeal for hospitality among believers.

The church in Rome was comprised of Gentile as well as Jewish Christian worshipers. Apparently conflicts had arisen among the members concerning the matter of importance and rank in the community of faith. Paul instructed the Gentile Christians not to think of themselves as superior to the Jewish Christians (Romans 11:18-20). In Romans 15:7, Paul reminded the believers that Christ receives all of them as children of God. So, both Jews and Gentiles must cordially welcome

each other as equals in Christ. Paul admonished the members of the church at Rome to extend hospitality so that God's glory might be revealed. Brotherly and sisterly love produces harmony. Unity in the body of Christ allows others to see God's glory at work in the church.

Apparently the believers heeded Paul's words to welcome one another as expressed in Romans 15:7. When Paul arrived in Rome around A.D. 60, Christians met him on the Appian Way, a Roman road, welcomed him, and even accompanied him into the city, where Paul spent two years as a prisoner before his death.

Paul's teaching is relevant for us today as we enter our places of worship. Christian hospitality and welcome must be offered to all who enter our church doors, regardless of status, race, or gender. Due to their unbridled enthusiasm and vibrant energy, children possess the God-given gifts to welcome others. They need help in understanding ways to extend hospitality, especially in the worship setting. With instruction, practice, and training, children can gain confidence in their abilities to welcome others. Experiences of extending radical hospitality prepare children to more effectively engage in worship. Hospitable children welcome and invite the presence of God, just as their loving and compassionate hearts welcome and invite others to join them in worship.

 **Enter With Gladness**

As the Children Arrive

Supplies: *smiley face stickers*

- Greet each child by name. As each child enters, express gladness that he or she is present.

- Place a smiley face sticker on each child's hand or clothing.

Make Hospitality Cards

Supplies: *markers or crayons, stickers, construction paper*

- As the children arrive, have them make cards for newer members of the congregation or recent visitors.

- Be sure to include any children whose families have recently joined or visited the church.

- Instruct the children to fold pieces of construction paper in half.

- Let the child decorate the front of his or her card with markers or crayons.

- Help the child write a short message of welcome inside the card. Mail the cards.

Visit the Worship Center

Supplies: *Bible, pictures of persons extending hospitality, a welcome banner or sign*

Preparation:

- *Set up a worship center on a small table. Cover the table with a cloth.*

- *Place some items in your worship center that represent hospitality. Display pictures of persons extending hospitality in the worship setting including shaking hands, greeting one another, hugging one another, accepting a new member, or baptizing a baby. Hang a welcome banner or sign in your worship area.*

- Visit the worship center. Show the children the pictures of persons showing hospitality to one another in the worship setting.

- Let the children talk about what is happening in each picture and in what way hospitality is being expressed.

 Bible Praise Notes

Supplies: *Bible, new member*

- Invite a new member of your church to visit the class. Ask him or her to share ways the church extended hospitality to him or her as a visitor and now as a new member.

- Let the new member read Romans 15:7 for the children: "*So welcome each other, in the same way that Christ also welcomed you, for God's glory.*"

- Have the children repeat the Bible verse several times.

- Have the children say the Bible verse to one another as they:

  Shake hands with other children.
  Pat other children on the back.
  Stand back to back with a partner.
  Wave to others in the class.
  Stand arm in arm with a partner.

Bible Verse Balloon Pop

Supplies: *balloons, large plastic bags, masking tape*

Preparation:

- *Blow up and tie balloons, one for each pair of students. Prepare balloons ahead of time and put in a large plastic garbage bag to bring to class.*

- *Use masking tape to make a long line on the floor in an open area.*

- Divide the class into pairs. If you have an odd number of students, recruit a youth volunteer or adult volunteer to pair with the extra chid.

- Have the pairs stand on opposite sides of the masking tape.

- Give one child in each pair an inflated balloon. Have the children tap the balloon back and forth across the line to each other, repeating the words *"Welcome each other, in the same way Christ welcomed you"* several times.

 # Let's Learn to Worship

Visitor Welcome Cards

Supplies: Reproducible 17—p. 112, *scissors*

Preparation:

- *Photocopy and cut apart "Visitor Welcome Cards" (Reproducible 17) for each child.*

- Divide the children into pairs and have them sit at a table or on the floor. Give each pair two sets of the cards.

- Have the pairs turn the cards face-down. Instruct the children to take turns drawing a card. Have the children share what is happening in the picture and in what way the persons are being welcomed in the church as a visitor.

Ask: Have you ever seen this sign of welcome happening in our church?

- If so, have the children place the card face-up. If not, have them to bring the card to you.

- After the game is over, show the children the cards they have given you. Talk with the children about ways to welcome others.

- Let the children share ways they see welcome taking place in the picture.

Ask: What are some ways our church could improve in welcoming others?

- Make a list of the children's answers. Share the children's concerns with your church staff.

Children Welcome Others

Supplies: *chairs, bulletin, welcome bag or children's worship bag*

Preparation:

- *Place the children in chairs as if they are gathered in your church's worship service.*

- Select a child to pretend be a visitor to the church. Have the visitor enter.

- Teach the children how to welcome the visitor.

- Have one child get up and say "hello" to the child, telling the child his or her name.

- Have one child give the visitor a bulletin, welcome bag, or children's worship bag, if you have those in your church.

- Have one child tell the visitor what will happen during the children's sermon, if your church has this time for children in your worship service.

- Have one child tell the visitor about children's worship, if your church offers this.

- Have one child tell the visitor about the activities your church offers children.

- Have one child introduce the child to some of his or her friends.

- Have the children role-play their parts several times with different children taking various roles. Let the children practice all of the roles at one time with a pretend visitor.

- Encourage children to watch for children who visit the church and be willing to go speak to them and welcome them.

- Remind the children to gain their parents' permission to welcome a child visitor.

Gift Bags for Children Visitors

Supplies: *paper bag with handles, crayons, markers, gift items for bags (pencils, small box of crayons, religious novelty items, stickers), pamphlet on children's activities in the church, CD of children's musical program or a CD of children's worship music*

- Let the children decorate and assemble welcome bags to be given to children who visit your church.

- Encourage the children to decorate the bags with crayons or markers.

- After the bags are decorated, have the children place the gift items in the bags.

- Find ways to let your children hand the bags out to visiting children as a way to welcome children to your church.

- If your church does not have many children visitors, you might also consider decorating and assembling bags for adult and youth visitors.

- Place materials in the visitor bag that gives information about church events, activities, and worship schedules.

- Have the children write welcoming notes or draw welcoming pictures.

Are Children Welcomed?

Supplies: *posterboard, marker, tape*

Preparation:

- *Draw a dividing line down the side of a piece of posterboard. On the left side of the dividing line, write the word "Welcomed." On the right side of the dividing line, write the words "Not Welcomed."*

Ask: What are some ways you feel welcomed by the congregation when you're in worship?

- Write the children's responses on the posterboard.

Ask: What are some ways you feel unwelcomed by the congregation when you're in worship?

- Write the children's responses on the posterboard.

Some things to consider:

Are children allowed to sign the attendance pads?

Are children occasionally used as worship leaders?

Do adults greet children?

Do children have their own worship bags?

Do ushers and worshipers pass the offering plate to children or skip over them?

Does your church have acolytes and does your church offer training?

Does your pastor take time to greet children as well as adults?

- Share with your church staff any ways that children feel welcomed or unwelcomed in the worship service.

Welcome Games

- Divide the children into several groups. Have them form a circle in their groups and stand close to each other.

- When you name something that applies to certain children (such as color of hair or eyes, grade in school, age, short, or tall), have those children step out of their group.

- Encourage the other groups to try and lure children into their groups as they shout, "Welcome!" or as they make hand motions to welcome others. Remind the children that it takes all of us to welcome others.

- Divide children into two teams. Have them form two lines, facing each other.

- Have the two lines approach each other and walk down the line shaking hands as they say, "Welcome" to each child they pass.

We Worship God

Welcome and Worship

Supplies: *white cloth, scissors, permanent marker,* The United Methodist Hymnal, *singer*

Preparation:

- *Cut strips of white cloth, one for each child.*

- *Use a permanent marker to write the word "Welcome" on each strip of cloth.*

- *Recruit a singer to teach the children some hymns from "The United Methodist Hymnal."*

- Give each child a strip of cloth. Show them the word *Welcome* on their cloth.

- Show the children how to tie the ends of the cloth together to make a circle.

- Have the children exchange their cloths with a friend. As they exchange their cloths, let the children say to one another, "You are welcome."

- Ask the singer to sing hymn 666. "Shalom to You," as the children wave their cloths to the music. Explain that the word *shalom* means "peace." Have the children sing the chorus.

- Have the children take their cloth and place it around the neck of a friend. As they do this, have them say, "You are welcome in worship."

- Ask the singer to sing hymn 558, "We are the Church." When the singer sings the word *church* have the children wave their cloth in the air.

- After the song is finished, have the children toss their piece of cloth into the air and catch it as they shout, **"We are welcomed in worship."**

- Instruct the children to untie their piece of cloth. Ask the singer to sing hymn 557, "Blest Be the Tie that Binds."

- As the hymn is sung, let each child tie his or her piece of cloth to another child's cloth. Continue tying until you form one large piece of cloth.

- Stretch the cloth out. Have volunteers hold the ends of the cloth.

- Invite the children to touch a part of the cloth as

they sing a favorite worship song.

- Place the cloth on your worship center and ask the children to say Romans 15:7.

We Welcome Others Invitation

Supplies: Reproducible 18—p. 113, Leaders' Guide—p. 66, *crayons*

Preparation:

- *Photocopy "My Family Helps Me Worship" (p. 66) for each child.*

- *Photocopy three copies of "Invitation" (Reproducible 18) for each child.*

- Give each child three copies of "Invitation."

- If time permits, let the children color their invitations. If not, encourage them to color their invitations at home.

- Encourage the children to use these invitations to welcome others to sit with them in worship.

- Suggest to the children that they invite church members of different ages to sit with them in the worship service. One week, ask them to invite an adult to sit with them. Another week, encourage them to invite a youth to sit with them. In the following week, ask them to invite a child.

Say: Be sure to share your invitations with your parents and gain your parent's approval for the persons you wish to invite to sit with you in the worship service.

Pray: God, you welcome us to worship. Help us welcome others. We can welcome visitors. We can greet our church friends. We can sit with someone who is lonely and needs a friend. When we welcome others, we remember that Jesus welcomed the little children and blessed them. Amen.

- Send *"My Family Helps Me Worship"* home with each child.

 # My Family Helps Me Worship

We Worship and We Welcome:

Your child learned about the Christian concept of hospitality. Your child received three invitations. We encourage your child, with your support, to invite an adult, a youth, and a child to sit with your family at three separate worship times. We're hopeful you will discuss this with your child and identify persons in the three age categories who need the welcome your child and family can offer.

Talk Points for the Week

Ask: What are some ways you feel welcomed at worship? What are some ways you feel unwelcomed at worship?

Say: Show me some ways you can welcome a child who is visiting our worship servce.

Family Worship

Set up a worship center in your home. Let the children in the family help you select a place for your worship center and items to place on your worship table.

How to Set Up Your Worship Center

1. Select a small table or card table.

2. Find a cloth to place on your center. Cover the table with the cloth. You might wish to select a cloth that is the color of the liturgical season.

3. Place symbols on your worship table that remind you of the concept of welcome. You might place a heart, a friendship bracelet, or a poster with the word *Welcome* written on it.

Worship God With Scripture

Blow up balloons, one for each family member. Teach the family Romans 15:7a.

Have family members say the verse together as they bop their balloons in the air.

Have family members say the verse as they bop their balloons in the air while turning in a circle.

Have family members toss the balloons to each other as they say the verse.

Sharing Ways to Welcome

Find out the names of new members who have recently joined or of persons who have recently visited your church. Provide note cards and let family members write a note of welcome to one or more of these friends. Let younger children draw a picture. Say a prayer for these persons.

Family Litany– Welcome to Worship

Use your balloons as you share in this family litany.

Leader: God welcomes us to worship.
Family: Yes! (Wave balloons in the air.)

Leader: God wants us to welcome others.
Family: Yes! (Exchange balloons with another family member.)

Leader: We welcome others with a handshake.
Family: Yes! (Family members shake hands with one another.)

Leader: We welcome others with a hug.
Family: Yes! (Family members hug one another.)

Leader: We welcome others with a "hello!"
Family: Yes! (Family members wave.)

Leader: We worship and we welcome.
Family: Yes! (Toss balloons in the air and catch.)

Prayer of Welcome

Prayer: Thank you, God, that we can worship. You welcome us! Help us reach out to others who visit our church and greet them. Help us welcome our new members and invite them to church events. Help us seek out persons in our congregation who are sad, lonely, or hurting and show love and kindness toward them. We pray as a family, and we ask this prayer in Jesus' name. Amen.

10 Children Have a Part in Worship

Bible Verses: There are different spiritual gifts but the same Spirit; and there are different ministries and the same Lord; and there are different activities but the same God who produces all of them in everyone.

(1 Corinthians 12:4-6)

Children will:

- Examine the Bible verses.
- Explore their God-given gifts and talents.
- Learn ways they can use their gifts to serve in worship.
- Identify worship roles for children in worship.

 # Worship Wisdom

The apostle Paul founded the church at Corinth. He spent nearly two years in the city ministering among the Christian converts. First Corinthians was written around A.D. 55. Paul composed this letter in the city of Ephesus, where he was ministering at that time. Paul sent his coworker Timothy to Corinth to deliver the letter and to set the church straight with some problems it was experiencing.

Corinth was a thriving city, both commercially and politically. As the capital of the province of Achaia, Corinth was a city of social, cultural, and religious diversity, including a Jewish community. In A.D. 49, the Jews were expelled from Rome. Many of them migrated to Corinth. Among these were Aquila and Priscilla, who became key leaders of the young Christian church and also became Paul's trusted friends and coworkers. Around 150-200 Christians were in Corinth at the time Paul wrote to them. They worshiped in house churches.

In 1 Corinthians 12, Paul wrote about spiritual gifts. Paul recognized that it was tempting to lift some gifts above others. Certain misguided persons claimed that their specific gifts were more important than the gifts of others. Paul sought to correct this false teaching. Paul believed that all gifts came from the Holy Spirit and were given by God. We learn from Paul that gifts are to be used for the good of the body of Christ.

God blesses our children with gifts, which are given to them by the Holy Spirit. We should encourage children to use their gifts and talents in ministry. Congregations must affirm the gifts of children and find ways to allow children to use their gifts in worship. Furthermore, congregations must intentionally seek out ways to allow children to serve as worship leaders. Congregations that are willing to let children serve recognize that children have the ability to use their talents. They affirm these gifts as the workings of the Holy Spirit. Children grow in their faith when they can participate fully in worship. Congregations receive a blessing when the gifts of children are recognized, affirmed, and used. Congregations that deny children the opportunity to serve miss out on the freshness, enthusiasm, vulnerability, humility, and passion that children bring to worship leadership.

You are given the awesome task of helping children discover their gifts for ministry. The discovery by our children of their God-given, spirit-breathed gifts can result in children stepping forth with confidence to use their gifts to serve the body of Christ.

Enter With Gladness

As the Children Arrive:

- Greet each child by name. As each child enters, express gladness that he or she is present.

- As the child enters the doorway of the classroom, stop him or her.

Ask: What is one of your talents? What do you do well?

Say: Praise God for (name of child) and his or her talent.

Draw a Picture

Supplies: *paper, crayons or markers*

Say: God gives children many talents.

Ask: What's one way you serve in church? *(acolyte, sing in children's choir, play hand bells).*

- If the child cannot name anything, ask him or her to think about a talent he or she possesses.

Say: A talent is something we do well and can use to serve others.

- Encourage each child to draw a picture showing a way he or she serves the church or draw a picture of his or her talent.

- Display the pictures on your worship altar.

Visit the Worship Center.

Supplies: *Bible, acolyte candlelighter, acolyte robe, children's choir robe, children's hand bell, pictures of children leading in worship, CD of children's cantata or play, drawings made earlier*

Preparation:

- *Set up a worship center on a small table. Cover the table with a cloth.*

- *Place on the table some items used in your worship service that represent the gifts and talents of children in your congregation.*

- Talk with the children about ways they serve God in the worship service. Have them share about ways they serve.

Bible Praise Notes

Learn the Bible Verses

Supplies: *Bible*

- Read 1 Corinthians 12:4-6 to the children.

Say: The apostle Paul wrote our Scripture verses. Paul wanted us to know that God gives us many talents. A talent is something you do very well. *(Give examples.)* No one's talent is better than another. God wants us to use our talents to serve others and help others worship God.

- Read the Bible verses to the children once again. When you say the word *different*, have them sit down. When you say the word *same*, have them stand up.

A Visit From the Apostle Paul

Supplies: *actor, Bible-times costume*

Preparation:

- *Recruit an individual to play the role of the apostle Paul. Dress him in a biblical-times costume.*

- Have Paul visit the class and share with the children about using their gifts to serve God. Encourage him to memorize the script.

Script for Apostle Paul

Hello, Boys and Girls. Let me introduce myself. I'm the apostle Paul. I wrote many of the letters you find in your Bible. One of these is First Corinthians. In that letter, you will find the Scripture verses for your worship session. Your teacher has read the verses to you. I want to tell you why I wrote that verses of Scripture.

I wrote the verses of Scripture to the Christians in the city of Corinth. Some of the believers in the city thought that one talent was better than another. I wanted to be sure they understood that God gives each of us gifts, but no single gift is greater than another. All gifts are special. All gifts come from God. We should use our gifts to help others worship God.

God has given you many gifts. Some of you are acolytes. You serve the church by lighting candles that remind worshipers that Jesus is the light of the world. Some of you sing in the children's choir. You sing beautiful songs that help worshipers praise God. Some of you play hand bells. You play music, and people who listen worship God through your music. Some of you like to read Scripture. God gave you a good reading voice, and you remind the worshipers that God has a message for us in the Bible. All of these gifts are very important.

Some of you have talents such as playing sports, playing music, dancing, gymnastics, art, poetry, or writing. Whatever your talent, share it gladly with others. Use your talent to honor God.

 # Let's Learn to Worship

Serving God Picture Card Game

Supplies: Reproducible 19—p. 114, *scissors*

Preparation:

- *Photocopy "Serving God" (Reproducible 19) for each child.*

- Give each child "Serving God." Have each child cut out the picture cards and place them in a stack, face-down.

- Let the children choose partners.

Say: Both of you draw a card. If the cards you are holding match, talk about how the child in the picture is serving the church. Then lay those cards aside. If the cards do not match, insert them back into your stack of cards.

- Keep playing until the children have matched all of their cards.

God Gave Me Talents

Supplies: *mirrors*

- Give each child a mirror. Have the children hold their mirrors in their laps.

Say: I'm going to say some words. If the word describes you, look into your mirror. If the word does not describe you, keep your mirror in your lap.

Words: quiet, curious, welcomes people, friendly, cheerful, likes music, shares with others, helps willingly, plays a musical instrument, kind, ballplayer, acolyte, Bible reader, great smile, happy, strong, likes animals, likes math, patient, likes plants, gentle, helps in worship

Stand Up and Take a Bow

- Name some of the ways children serve in your church.

- When you name a certain service, ask all of the children that serve in this way to stand up and bow.

- Have the other children clap for them as a way of expressing thanks and praise.

- Remind the children that they are bowing, not to receive praise, but, rather, bowing before God who gave them the talent.

I Spy Talent Bottles

Supplies: *clean plastic bottles with lids; small erasers that represent talents (football, soccer, music note); small pictures of various talents (children may wish to draw these); small miniature items that represent talents; small square pieces of paper; plastic craft pellets or other filler options such as birdseed, sand, or plastic pellets; ribbon*

- Give each child a plastic bottle and allow him or her to select several items to place in the plastic bottle.

- Encourage each child to draw a picture on a few small square pieces of paper to represent his or her talent. Have the child add the paper to the bottle.

- The children do not have to put items in the bottle that represent just their talents, but the talents of friends as well.

- Help each child pour some of the filler material in the bottle.

- Then let the children drop more of the objects in their bottles.

- Repeat until all the items are in the bottle. Only fill the bottle about ¾ full, as the objects need room to mix around and move.

- Glue the lids in place using strong glue.

- Help each child tie a ribbon around the lid for decoration.

- Once the glue has dried, the children can gently shake and rotate the bottle to try to find the objects.

Talents Game

Supplies: *large container or plastic bag; items that represent the talents of children such as a football, a basketball, ballet slippers, a dance trophy, a soccer ball, a scholastic award, an attendance certificate, an acolyte pin, an acolyte robe, a choir robe, a hand bell*

Preparation:

- *Place the items in a large container or large plastic bag.*

- Select one item and hold it up for the children to view.

- The first child to shout the word "Talent!" is allowed to guess what talent the item represents. If that child correctly identifies the talent, he or she gets to hold the item and is not allowed to guess again.

- Continue the game until all the items have been selected.

- Spread the items out around your classroom. Let the children go and stand beside an item that represents his or her talent.

- After a few moments, allow the children to switch and go to another location that represents another talent. If children do not have other talents represented by the items you selected, ask them to remain in place and to welcome new children as they arrive.

- Have children switch places several times.

- Affirm the talents and gifts of the children.

 # We Worship God

Affirming Our Talents

- Have the children take turns calling out one of their talents. Especially encourage the children to share about ways they serve in the church.

- After each child shares a talent, have the class respond, "Thanks be to God!"

God Gifts Children

Say: Your talents are gifts given to you by God. You can use your talents to honor God and to serve others.

- Divide the children into group of 3-5 persons. Whisper a talent to each group. Give the groups a few minutes to plan how to act out the talent.

- Have each group act out the talent for the other children.

- Have the other children guess what talent the group is acting out.

Ask: How can this talent be used to worship God?

Ideas of talents to whisper to the children:
play sport (name individual sports), play musical instrument (name individual instruments), dance, sing, play hand bells, do gymnastics, swim, write, draw, read, write poetry, read Scripture, usher, acolyte, sing in children's choir, drama

Share Our Talents

Supplies: Leaders' Guide—p. 72

Preparation:

- *Photocopy "My Family Helps Me Worship" (p. 72) for each child.*

- *Photocopy the Bible reading printed below.*

Say: Let's use our talents now to worship God.

- Ask for four volunteers who have a talent for reading to read the Bible reading below. Reader 2 has the most lines.

- Ask for a volunteer who has a talent for singing to sing a simple praise song such as "Jesus Loves Me," "If You're Happy and You Know It," or one of their own choosing.

Say: Let's name everyone in our group who has a talent.

- Ask for a volunteer who has a talent for sports to lead the children in a game. Have the children stand in a circle. Give the child chosen to be the leader a ball. Have the child toss the ball to someone in the circle and say the child's name.

Then have the child toss the ball back to the leader. Have the leader continue around the circle until everyone has been named.

Say: God gives each one of us gifts and talents.

- Lead the children in the following litany.

Leader: Thank you, God, for children who play sports and are good sports.

Children: Amen.

Leader: Thank you, God, for children who play music and sing praises to You.

Children: Amen.

Leader: Thank you, God, for children who dance or do gymnastics. You created their bodies.

Children: Amen.

Leader: Thank you, God, for children who study hard and do well in school.

Children: Amen.

Leader: Thank you, God, for children who are artists, poets, or writers.

Children: Amen.

Leader: Thank you, God, for children who are acolytes, who sing in the choir, who play hand bells, or who serve in other ways in our church.

Children: Amen.

Leader: Thank you, God, for the ways children use their talents in worship. Help each child use his or her talents to honor you and serve others.

Children: Amen.

- Send "My Family Helps Me Worship" home with each child.

Bible Reading

Reader 1: There are different spiritual gifts

Reader 2: but the same Spirit;

Reader 3: and there are different ministries

Reader 2: and the same Lord;

Reader 4: and there are different activities

Reader 2: but the same God who produces all of them in everyone.
(1 Corinthians 12:4-6)

 # My Family Helps Me Worship

Children Have a Part in Worship

In our worship session, children learned about ways they can use their talents to serve God, particularly in the worship service. We explored the talents of the children in our church, affirmed these talents, and reminded the children to use them to serve God and others.

Talk Points for the Week

Ask: How do you serve the church?

Affirm the gifts of your child and his or her service.

Ask: What are your talents?

Remind your child that these talents are gifts from God. Take time to thank God for your child's talents and gifts.

Family Worship

Set up a worship center in your home. Let the children in the family help you select a place for your worship center and items to place on your worship table.

How to Set Up Your Worship Center

1. Select a small table or card table.

2. Find a cloth to place on your center. Cover the table with the cloth. You might wish to select a cloth that is the color of the liturgical season.

3. Place some items on your table that represent the talents of your family members.

Affirm and Give Thanks for Talents

Gather around the worship center and look at the items that symbolize the talents of family members.

Affirm each other and offer praise to God for the gifts God has given each member of the family.

Read 1 Corinthians 12:4-6.

Remind family members that God gives us gifts. Family members may have different gifts, but they all come from God's Spirit. No one gift is better than another. All gifts are important and valuable. Gifts and talents should be used to honor God.

Family Talent and Worship Time

Plan a family talent and worship time. Encourage each member of the family to share one or more talent as a part of your worship time. Make this a worshipful time.

If your child is an acolyte at church, allow him or her to light candles to begin your family talent and worship time.

If a family member has a musical talent, ask him or her to play or sing some worship music.

If a family member has a talent at writing or drawing, have him or her write a letter to God or draw a religious picture.

If a family member is a dancer, have him or her dance to worship music.

If a family member plays sports, have him or her share a story about how he or she has learned to share or exhibit good sportsmanship or share about lessons learned from his or her coach.

If a family member sews, knits, crochets, or makes crafts, have that family members display his or her handiwork.

If a family member cooks or bakes, have him or her make the family a treat to enjoy after the worship service is concluded.

Have each family member hold an item from your worship altar that represents his or her talent.

Prayer: Say a prayer for each family member by name, giving God thanks for that person's God-given talent.

Worship the Lord With Gladness: God's Children in Worship

11 Special Times of Worship: The Church Seasons

Bible Verse: There's a season for everything and a time for every matter under the heavens. (*Ecclesiastes 3:1*)

Children will:

• Examine the Bible verse.

• Learn about the church seasons.

• Explore the ways the church seasons are used in worship.

• Think about ways the seasons of their own lives intersect with the church seasons.

 # Worship Wisdom

Ecclesiastes is a part of the biblical books known as Wisdom Literature. Among these books found in our Bibles are Job, Psalms, Proverbs, and Song of Songs. These biblical writings offer insights and wisdom about everyday living in accordance with God's laws and purposes.

The authorship of the Book of Ecclesiastes is attributed to King Solomon, but scholars are uncertain exactly who wrote the book. The author identifies himself with the Hebrew title of *Qoheleth*. This is the title given to an official speaker who calls an assembly together. The author also refers to himself as the Teacher. This lets us know that, regardless of who wrote the Book of Ecclesiastes, the author was a respected leader in the Jewish tradition.

The Hebrew title *Qoheleth* carries with it the idea of debating. In Ecclesiastes, the author is not so much debating with the listeners but arguing with himself. The author presents a topic, discusses it from many viewpoints, and finally, comes to a practical conclusion.

In Ecclesiastes 3:1, the sage reminds us that from the moment we are born to the moment we die, our lives are limited and dictated by time. There is a beginning and an end to every human pursuit and endeavor. The author understands that life is not an endless, meaningless existence; instead life offers each person an orderly, purposeful

arrangement. The author believes that God has a plan and a purpose for our experiences of daily living and our seasons of worship. All of time remains in God's hands, and there is an appropriate time for every human activity.

The church seasons offer us an understanding of time in relationship to our worship and praise of God. The church seasons help us recognize the holy times of life, as God invades our space. God permeates our lives with God's amazing grace and abundant love. Yet, God is present with us not only in the special and holy times of life but also in the mundane, ordinary events of everyday living.

As children explore the church seasons, they will gain a greater understanding of the importance of time in the church. They will recognize that the church seasons help them worship God and, furthermore, teach them about the life of Jesus. They will also come to the realization that God is present with them and faithful to them in all seasons of their lives. God is with them in the holy and special moments of their lives, just as God is an abiding presence in the everyday experiences of life.

Children learn through repetition. The church seasons, with their repetitive cycles, offer children an opportunity to praise God that takes into account their need for repetition as a helpful and vitally effective way of learning and worshiping.

 **Enter With Gladness**

As the Children Arrive:

Supplies: *clocks, watches, cell phone, stoles*

Preparation:

- *Borrow stoles from your pastor or another pastor that represent the different seasons of the church year.*

- Greet each child by name. As each child enters, express gladness that he or she is present.

- Have clocks and watches for the children to look at as they enter the room. Show the children what time it is using a cell phone and the clocks.

Say: We have many ways to tell time today. We also have a way to tell time in the church through the church seasons. The church seasons teach us about the life of Jesus. The church seasons help us worship. We use different colors in our church to represent the different church seasons.

- Show the children the stoles, and let them identify the colors used in the church seasons.

- Remind the children that many pastors wear stoles in worship.

Say: The stole the pastor wears helps us know what season it is on the church calendar. Each color is used twice, except for the red color, which is used only once.

- Encourage the children to look at the color of the stoles their pastors wear (if they wear a stole in worship) and also to look at the color of the paraments (cloths on the altar, pulpit, and lectern).

Color a Stole

Supplies: Reproducible 20—p. 115, *purple crayons, white crayons, green crayons, red crayons*

Preparation:

- *Photocopy "Stoles for the Church Year" (Reproducible 20) for each child.*

- Give each child "Stoles for the Church Year."

Ask: Which stole reminds you of Advent, the time when we get ready to celebrate Jesus' birth? *(the stole with the candles/stars)*

Say: The color for Advent is purple.

- Have the children color the Advent stole purple.

Ask: Which stole reminds you of Christmas, the time when we remember Jesus' birth? *(the stole with the mother and child)*

Say: The color for the Christmas season is white.

- Have the children color the Christmas stole white.

Ask: Which stole reminds you of Lent, the time when we remember that Jesus died on the cross? *(the stole with the cross)*

Say: The color for Lent is purple.

- Have the children color the Lent stole purple.

Ask: Which stole reminds you of Easter, the time when we remember that Jesus rose again? *(the stole with "Alleluia")*

Say: The color for Easter is white.

- Have the children color the Easter stole white.

Ask: Which stole reminds you of Pentecost, the time when we remember the coming of the Holy Spirit? *(the stole with the dove)*

Say: The color for Pentecost is red.

- Have the children color the Pentecost stole red.

Ask: Which stole reminds you of Ordinary Time, the time when we remember that we try to follow Jesus every day? *(the stole with the sign of the fish)*

Say: The color for Ordinary Time is green.

- Have the children color the Ordinary time stole green.

Say: We're missing one stole, the stole for Epiphany. That's when we remember the wise men who followed the star to find Jesus. The color for Epiphany is green.

Ask: What do you think should be the symbol on a stole for Epiphany? *(a star)*

View the Worship Center

Supplies: *Advent wreath, chrismons, manger, wise men, crown, star, gifts, cross, donkey, palm leaf, pitcher/basin, eggs, lilies, church, dove, clock, calendar*

Preparation:

- *Set up a worship center on a small table. Cover the table with overlapping cloths to symbolize the various colors of the church seasons (purple, white, green, red).*

- *Place on the table some items that represent the seasons of the church year.*

- Show the children the items on your worship center.

Say: Each item helps us learn about a church season.

- Name each church season, and let the children repeat the name of the church season after you. Briefly tell the children what each church season means.

Advent—We prepare for the birth of Jesus.

Christmas—We celebrate the birth of Jesus.

Epiphany—We learn about the wise men who visited Jesus.

Lent—We learn about the of Jesus and his death on the cross.

Easter—We learn that Jesus is alive!

Pentecost—We learn about the birthday of the church.

Ordinary Time—We learn that God is with us all of the time, even in the ordinary events of everyday living.

- Name some ordinary events that children encounter in their lives such as: eating meals, playing, watching television, working on the computer, going to the doctor, going to school, walking the dog. When you name an event, have the children respond: "God is with me!"

 # Bible Praise Notes

Learn the Bible Verse

Supplies: *Bible, play watches*

- Help the children fasten their play watches on their wrists.

- Have them look at their watches as you read Ecclesiastes 3:1.

What Time Is It?

Supplies: dry erase board, dry erase markers or large sheets of paper, markers

Say: Name some ways you use your time during the week.

- List these on a dry erase board or large sheets of paper.

- Read each activity listed. When you read an activity, ask the children the question, "What time is it?

- Have the children look at their play watches and respond, "God's time!"

Ideas: I go to school. I go to church. I go to dance. I go to baseball practice. I go to soccer practice. I go to bed.

My Favorite Season

Supplies: *paper, crayons or markers, items that represent the seasons of the year, large container*

Preparation

- *Place the items that represent the seasons in a large container.*

Worship the Lord With Gladness: God's Children in Worship

- Let the children draw a picture of their favorite season in nature.

- Have the children share their drawings.

- After each child shares, read the Scripture verse from Ecclesiastes 3:1: "There's a season for everything and a time for every matter under the heavens."

Say: God is in charge of the seasons of the year.

- Divide the children into groups according to their favorite season in nature. Let the children take their drawings with them as they sit in their groups.

- Call out a season in nature and, ask the group of children gathered in that seasonal group to stand up. Tell them to sit down quickly when another season is called out.

- Repeat the names of the seasons (fall, winter, spring, summer) several times as the children stand up and then sit down.

- Show the children the container. Let a child from each seasonal group come forward and select an item that represents his or her favorite season. Have him or her return to the group with the item.

- Continue letting children select until each group has a variety of items that represent their favorite season of the year.

- Repeat the names of the seasons (fall, winter, spring, summer) again. Have the groups hold up the items they collected as you name each season.

Say: Just as there are seasons in nature, we have seasons in the church. These seasons help us learn about Jesus. In our worship session, we will learn about our church seasons.

 # Let's Learn To Worship

Church Year Clock

Supplies: Reproducible 21—p. 116, *posterboard, glue, brads, scissors, hole punch, crayons or markers*

Preparation:

- *Photocopy "Church Year Clock" (Reproducible 21) for each child.*

- *Cut from posterboard a slightly larger circle than the church year clock, one circle for each child.*

- Give each child "Church Year Clock." Have the child cut out the circle and the arrow.

- Give each child a posterboard circle and have him or her glue the church year clock on the circle.

- Help each child punch a hole in the arrow and show him or her how to attach a brad to the arrow. Then help the child attach his or her arrow to the clock by using the brad to punch a hole in the clock and attach.

- Call out the seasons of the church year. Have each child move his or her arrow to the corresponding word on the child's clock. Help children find the word for each church season, as you briefly tell the children about that church season.

Advent—We prepare for the birth of Jesus.

Christmas—We celebrate the birth of Jesus.

Epiphany—We learn about the wise men who visited Jesus.

Lent—We learn about the life of Jesus and his death on the cross.

Easter—We learn that Jesus is alive!

Pentecost—We learn about the birthday of the church.

Ordinary Time—We learn that God is with us all of the time, even in the ordinary events of everyday living.

Make a Church Seasons Booklet

Supplies: *construction paper; 8½- by-11 inch white paper; purple, red, white, and green ribbons; crayons; markers; scissors; stapler; staples*

Preparation:

- *Make a booklet for each child. Fold the construction paper in half. Fold two sheets of the white paper int half. Staple the folded white sheets of paper inside the folded piece of construction paper to make eight panels.*

- *Cut pieces of purple, red, white, and green ribbons and attach together to the top edge of the booklet.*

- *Write the words My Church Seasons Booklet on the cover. Write the name of one of the church seasons on the top of each of the white pages in the booklet.*

- Give each child a booklet. Encourage the children to draw an appropriate symbol for each church season.

- Let the children take their church seasons booklets with them to your church's worship service and add symbols as they observe the ways your church uses the church seasons in worship.

Advent—Draw four candles for the four weeks of Advent and to represent the Advent wreath.

Christmas—Draw a picture of baby Jesus.

Epiphany—Draw a star to represent the wise men's visit to Jesus.

Lent—Draw a cross to remember Jesus.

Easter—Draw a picture of the empty tomb.

Pentecost—Draw a picture of a dove to represent the Holy Spirit.

Ordinary Time—Let the child draw a picture of a daily activity.

- Show the children how to use their ribbon bookmarks to place in page for a particular season of the church year that corresponds with the color of the ribbon.

Seasons in Sand

Supplies: *empty water bottles with tops; white, red, purple, and green sand; funnels; glue or tape*

- Give each child a bottle. Show him or her how to layer the colored sand in the bottle to represent the colors of the church seasons.

- Help the children place tops on the bottles and secure them with glue or tape.

Set Up a Seasons Fair

Supplies: *seven small tables or seven boxes; purple, white, green, and red paper or cloth; Advent wreath; Nativity set*

Preparation:

- *Set up seven stations in your room. You may use seven small tables, or seven boxes turned upside down.*

- Have the children help you set up each station. You may want to divide the children into work groups and have each group be responsible for a station.

- Station 1—Advent. Cover the table or box with purple paper or cloth. Add an Advent wreath.

- Station 2—Christmas. Cover the table or box with white paper or cloth. Add a Nativity set.

- Station 3—Epiphany. Cover the table or box with green paper or cloth. Add a crown or a star.

- Station 4—Lent. Cover the table or box with purple paper or cloth. Add a cross.

- Station 5—Easter. Cover the table or box with white paper or cloth. Add a butterfly or lily.

- Station 6—Pentecost. Cover the table or box with red paper or cloth. Add a birthday cake or cupcakes for the birthday of the church.

- Station 7—Ordinary Time. Cover the table or box with green paper or cloth. Add a calendar or clock.

We Worship God

Colorful Worship Parade

Supplies: Leaders' Guide—p. 79, *white, purple, red, and green crepe paper; scissors; stations set up earlier*

Preparation:

- *Photocopy "My Family Helps Me Worship" (p. 79) for each child.*

- *Cut white, purple, red, and green steamers long enough to go around the neck of each child.*

- Have the children place the streamers around their necks. Line them up for a parade.

- Have the children sing "Ecclesiastes 3:1" to the tune of "Do You Know the Muffin Man?" as they march around the room. End the parade at the Advent station.

Ecclesiastes 3:1

For everything there is a season,
is a season, is a season.
For everything there is a season;
God made them all.

- Have your children wave their purple streamers when they arrive at the Advent station.

Say: Purple is the color for Advent. Advent helps us prepare for the birth of Jesus.

- Have the children sing "Ecclesiastes 3:1" as they march to the Christmas station.

- Have the children wave their white streamers when they arrive at the Christmas station.

Say: White is the color for Christmas. Jesus was born at Christmas.

- Have the children sing "Ecclesiastes 3:1" as they march to the Epiphany station.

- Have the children wave their green streamers when they arrive at the Epiphany station.

Say: Green is the color for Epiphany. Epiphany helps us learn about the wise men. The wise men followed the star to Jesus.

- Have the children sing "Ecclesiastes 3:1" as they march to the Lent station.

- Have the children wave their purple streamers when they arrive at the Lent station.

Say: Purple is the color for Lent. We learn about Jesus during Lent. The cross reminds us of Jesus.

- Have the children sing "Ecclesiastes 3:1" as they march to the Easter station.

- Have the children wave their white streamers when they arrive at the Easter station.

Say: White is the color of Easter. At Easter, we celebrate the resurrection of Jesus.

- Have the children sing "Ecclesiastes 3:1" as they march to the Pentecost station.

- Have the children wave their red streamers when they arrive at Pentecost station.

Say: Red is the color of Pentecost. The church began at Pentecost. At Pentecost, we celebrate the birthday of the church.

- Let the children enjoy the birthday cake or cupcakes. (Check for allergies.)

- Have the children sing "Ecclesiastes 3:1" as they march to the Ordinary Time station.

- Have the children wave their green streamers when they arrive at the Ordinary Time station.

Say: Green is the color for ordinary time. Ordinary time reminds us that God is with us each day. No matter where we go or what we do, God is with us.

Pray: Thank you, God, for our church seasons. They teach us about Jesus. They help us worship God. We're glad that God is always with us, whatever the season in nature and whatever the season in our church. Amen.

- Send *"My Family Helps Me Worship"* home with each child.

 # My Family Helps Me Worship

Special Times of Worship: The Church Seasons

The United Methodist Church uses church seasons in our times of worship. The church seasons teach us about the life of Jesus. Your child learned about the church seasons of Advent, Christmas, Epiphany, Lent, Easter, Pentecost, and Ordinary Time.

Talk Points for the Week

Ask: What are the four seasons in nature? *(fall, winter, spring, summer)* What are some of the seasons in the church? *(Advent, Christmas, Epiphany, Lent, Easter, Pentecost, and Ordinary Time)*

Family Worship

Set up a worship center in your home Let the children in the family help you select a place for your worship center and items to place on your worship table.

How to Set Up Your Worship Center

1. Select a small table or card table.

2. Place streamers or pieces of cloth to represent the colors of the church seasons: white, purple, green, and red.

3. Place items on your table to represent the church seasons. (Advent—baby items; Christmas—Navitity set; Epiphany—wise men, star; Lent—cross; Eastertide—egg, lily; Pentecost—church, dove; Ordinary Time—clock, calendar, cell phone

Worship God With Scripture

- Read Ecclesiastes 3:1

- Have family members take turns naming an event or activity that he or she will engage in during the week. After each family member shares, have other family members respond with the words "God is with you."

The Church Seasons Help Us Worship

Let family members take turns pointing out items in your worship center that relate to a particular church season as you read a description of that church season for the family.

Advent	We prepare for the birth of Jesus.
Christmas	We celebrate the birth of Jesus.
Epiphany	We learn about the wise men who visited Jesus.
Lent	We learn about the life of Jesus and his death.
Easter	We learn that Jesus is alive!
Pentecost	We learn about the birthday of the church.
Ordinary Time	We learn that God is with us all of the time, even in the ordinary events of everyday living.

I Spy a Church Season Color

Place a game of "I Spy." Use the colors of the church seasons (red, purple, white, and green). Have a family member look for an item around the room that is the same color as a color used in the church seasons. Let other family members try to guess what the family member has spied. When a family member guesses correctly, that family member must name what church seasons uses that particular color. *(purple—Advent and Lent; white—Christmas and Easter; green—Epiphany and Ordinary Time; red—Pentecost)*

Sing Songs of the Church Seasons

Have family members sing some favorite songs about the life of Jesus, including Jesus' birth, ministry, death, and resurrection.

Tell a Story

Have a family member tell a story about Jesus.

Pray: Thank you, God, for the church seasons. They help our family worship God. We're glad our church uses the church seasons in worship to teach our family about the life of Jesus. Amen.

12. We Gather to Worship, We Leave to Serve

Bible Verses: Jesus replied, "The most important one is 'Israel, listen! Our God is the one Lord, and you must love the Lord your God with all your heart, with all your being, with all your mind, and with all your strength.' The second is this, 'You will love your neighbor as yourself.' No other commandment is greater than these." (*Mark 12:29-31*)

Children will:
- Examine the Bible verses.
- Explore ways to serve others.
- Think about the ways worship prepares them to serve others.
- Learn about ways of putting into practice the biblical concepts of sharing, caring, mission, and stewardship taught to them in worship.

Worship Wisdom

Jewish religious leaders often debated among themselves which commandment was the greatest. The Pharisees diligently studied the law and their ritual requirements. There were 616 precepts of the Old Testament along with numerous rabbinic commentaries. Knowledge of the law required a lifetime of devoted study. Although all commandments were equal in a sense, rabbis often reflected on which commandments held the greatest weight.

The Gospel of Mark records the incident involving the questioning of Jesus by a scribe. A scribe was recognized in Jewish tradition as a learned and educated teacher of the law. The man approached Jesus with a question about which commandment was the greatest. Probably this man wished to test Jesus to see if Jesus correctly understood the law in the same diligent and studious manner as this scribe believed that he did.

Jesus showed that he clearly understood the greatest commandment. He quoted from Deuteronomy 6:4-9. This passage, called the Shema, instructs the believer to love God in a passionate and devout manner. It is the best-known text of Judaism. Twice every day, in Jesus' time, the faithful Jew recited the Shema: "*Israel,*

listen! Our God is the LORD! Only the LORD! Love the LORD your God with all your heart, all your being, and all your strength." Yet, Jesus went further than the teaching of the Shema. He added a second commandment, inseparable from the first. Jesus borrowed a teaching from Leviticus 19:18 to inform the scribe that the second great commandment involved loving one's neighbor as oneself.

It is helpful to compare Jesus' teaching in Mark's Gospel with similar teachings in Matthew 22:37-40 and Luke 10:25-27. In Matthew's Gospel a lawyer questions Jesus. In Luke's gospel, a lawyer questions Jesus; here, in addition to the teachings about the two commandments, Jesus provides an example of neighbor. Jesus tells the story of the good Samaritan, not only in answer to the lawyer's question, "Who is my neighbor?" but also to demonstrate what love of neighbor actually entails. Jesus enlarges our vision and understanding of *neighbor* to be anyone in need.

True worship of God always leads to service, and children are called to serve. Like adult worshipers, they must be sent forth from worship with blessings over their gifts and with the admonition to use these gifts in service.

 # Enter With Gladness

Make a Mezuzah

Supplies: Reproducible 22—p. 117 (bottom), *shoebox, paper for scroll, yarn, plain paper, tape*

Preparation:

- *Photocopy and cut off the Shema (Reproducible 22).*

- *Crumple the paper and smooth it out again. Roll the paper into a scroll and tie with a piece of yarn.*

- *If the shoebox has writing on it, wrap the shoebox in plain paper.*

As the Children Arrive

Supplies: *scarf or Bible-times head covering, shoebox, crayons or markers, stickers, scroll made earlier*

- Give each child a scarf or head covering to wear.

Say: In Bible times a Jewish worshiper showed respect to God by wearing a covering on his or her head.

Say: Listen (name of child), our God is the one Lord. Love the Lord with all your heart and love others.

- Let the children work together to decorate the shoebox with crayons or markers and stickers.

- Show the children the scroll. Put the scroll in the shoebox.

Say: You have helped me make a mezuzah. A mezuzah is a special container with a scroll inside. In Bible times, the Jewish people wrote some words on the scroll to remind them to worship only God and to love God with their heart, soul, mind, and body. They called these important words the Shema. The mezuzah was placed on the doorpost of a house. The people would touch the mezuzah as they went in and out of the house.

- Open the mezuzah and unroll the scroll. Read the words to the children.

- Place the mezuzah at your door. Invite all the children to touch the mezuzah.

Say: Jesus would have touched a mezuzah at his house.

View the Worship Center

Supplies: *Bible, cloth, globe, schoolbooks, items to represent home*

Preparation:

- *Set up a worship center on a small table. Cover the table with a cloth.*

- *Place a globe on the table to represent the world and community. Place schoolbooks and other items on the table to represent the schools the children attend. Also place on the table some items to represent the homes of the children.*

- Show the children the items on your worship center.

Say: Today in our worship session we are going to learn ways to serve others. Worship helps us praise God, but in worship we also learn ways to love and care for others.

Ask: What are some ways you have shown love and care for others at school, in your neighborhood, or in the community? *(raked leaves for a neighbor; walked a friend's dog; visited a sick friend; sent cards to a sick church friend; sat with a newcomer during lunch at school; collected food, clothes or toys for those in need; congratulated members of an opposing sports team when they have played well; been a good sport in competitive sports, dance, or gymnastics; recycled; picked up trash; put out a bird feeder to provide food for the birds)*

Bible Praise Notes

Learn the Bible Verses

Supplies: *Bible; shofar, bell, or other instrument*

- Read the first part of the Mark 12:29-31 to the children:

Jesus replied, "The most important one is 'Israel, listen! Our God is the one Lord and you must love the Lord your God with all your heart, with all your being, with all your mind, and with all your strength.'"

Say: These words are called the Shema. Jesus would have learned these words when he was a young boy. In our Bible verses for today, Jesus taught that it is important to love God with our bodies, our minds, and our hearts. We worship God with our whole beings!

- Let the children practice saying this verse together several times.

- Prior to saying the verse, have a volunteer say: "Israel, listen!" When those words are said, blow a shofar (Jewish horn that calls the people to worship), ring a bell, or play some instrument to get the attention of the children. Then, have them say the verse.

- Divide the children into four groups: heart, being, mind, and strength.

- Have all the children say the verse together, but have the groups jump up when they hear the key word for their group.

- Teach the children motions to use when they say the Shema:

- When they say the word *heart*—have them draw a heart in the air with their fingers.

- When they say the word *being*—have them wiggle their bodies.

- When they say the word *mind*—have them point to their heads.

- When they say the word *strength*—have them flex their muscles.

Read the second part of Mark 12:29-31 to the children:

The second is this, "You will love your neighbor as yourself. No other commandment is greater than these."

Say: Jesus not only told the people to love God, but to love others.

Un-jumble the Words

Supplies: Reproducible 22—p. 117 (top), *pencils*

Preparation:

- *Photocopy "Unscramble the Verse" (Reproducible 22) for each child.*

- Give each child "Unscramble the Verse." Have the children unscramble the words and write them in the spaces provided.

Let's Learn to Worship

Make a Mezuzah

Supplies: Reproducible 22—p. 117 (bottom), *scissors, jewelry-size gift boxes, stick-on jewels or other stickers, yarn, crayons or markers*

Preparation:

- *Photocopy and cut off the Shema (Reproducible 22) for each child.*

- Give each child a jewelry-size gift box. Have the child decorate the outside of the jewelry box with stick-on jewels or other stickers.

- Give each child the Shema and a piece of yarn. Let the children decorate around the words with crayons or markers.

- Have the children crumple the paper into a ball and then spread it out again. Repeat this process several times. This will make the paper look like old leather.

- Show the children how to roll the paper printout of the Shema into a scroll. Have each child tie his or her scroll with a piece of yarn and place inside the decorated box.

Say: In Bible times, Jewish people put the mezuzah on the doorposts of their homes. Whenever they went in or out of their homes, they touched the mezuzah.

- Encourage the children to show their mezuzahs to their family.

Have You Heard?

Say: If we're listening, we can learn about ways to serve others while we're in our church worship service. Listen to what I say. If what I say is something you've heard in worship, stand up. If you have not heard it in worship, sit down.

- Say the statements printed below. Let the children stand up and sit down.

Say: Our pastor preached a sermon about sharing.

Our youth went on a mission trip and talked about it in worship.

Our church planned a mission project and talked about in worship.

We sing songs and hymns in our worship service that teach us about sharing.

Our prayers teach us to serve others.

Our worship leaders, ushers, acolytes, and musicians set examples for us on ways to serve others.

 # We Worship God

Paint and Worship

Supplies: *Bible, praise CD, CD player, smocks, washable paint, paintbrushes, small paper plates, bowls of water for cleaning brushes, paper or plastic tablecloth*

Preparation:

- *Squeeze out different colors of paint and place on small paper plates. Provide bowls of water for cleaning paintbrushes.*

- *Cover the table with paper or plastic.*

- Have the children wear smocks. Invite the children to sit down at the table.

- Give each child a paintbrush. Before painting, have the children close their eyes. Read Mark 12:29-31 to the children.

- Let the children continue to close their eyes and think about what they will paint as a way to worship God.

- Play quiet music as the children paint. Instruct the children that there is to be no talking or laughing. Their painting time is to be a time of worship.

- After the children finish painting, lay the pictures aside to dry.

- Encourage the children to give their paintings as a caring gift.

The Story of the Good Samaritan

Supplies: *Bible*

- Tell or read the parable of the Good Samaritan found in Luke 10:30-37.

Say: The Levite and priest were religious leaders during the time of Jesus. A Samaritan was not Jewish, but of another race. Samaritans and Jews were enemies.

Ask: Who turned out to be the neighbor in the story? *(Samaritan)* Why was it a surprise for the listeners of this story to learn that the Samaritan helped a Jewish man? *(Samaritans and Jews were enemies. They did not get along.)* Who is your neighbor today? *(Anyone who has a need.)*

Breaking News Skit

Supplies: Leaders' Guide—p. 85

Preparation:

- *Photocopy "Breaking News" (Leaders' Guide— p. 85) for each child participating in the skit. You will need seven copies.*

- Recruit volunteers to act out the skit "Breaking News!" based upon the Bible story of the good Samaritan. You may want to use adults or teens if the skit is above your children's reading level.

Sing About Neighbors

Supplies: The United Methodist Hymnal *or CD of* The United Methodist Hymnal, *CD player*

- Teach the children the chorus to "Jesus, Jesu" (*The United Methodist Hymnal*, 432).

Say: *Jesu* is another word for Jesus.

- Invite a singer to sing verses two and three of the hymn. After each verse, stop singing, and let the children identify their neighbors.

Say: Neighbors do not have to just live in your neighborhood. Neighbors be anyone in need.

How Can I Serve?

Supplies: Leaders' Guide—p. 86

Preparation:

- *Photocopy "My Family Helps Me Worship" (p. 86) for each child.*

- Divide the children into groups. Give each group one of the following scenarios. Have the group decide on a way to help in each situation.

- Share the scenarios with the entire group, and let each group share the ways they could help.

- Set a worshipful tone for the sharing by gathering the children around the worship center as they share.

Group One: You see a child at school being bullied by another child.

Group Two: You notice that a new child at school has no friends and seems very lonely.

Group Three: You and your family observe many homeless people on the streets in the town where you live.

Group Four: Your elderly neighbor lives alone and is in poor health.

Group Five: A child in your classroom is in the hospital.

- As each group offers suggestions on ways to help, have all of the children respond: "This is my neighbor!"

Pray: Thank you, God, for worship. Worship helps us praise you, but worship also teaches us to serve others. Jesus taught us that our neighbors are people in need. Help us to serve our neighbors. We offer our prayer in the name of Jesus. Amen.

- Send "My Family Helps Me Worship" home with each child.

Breaking News

Characters: *Joe Cool Reporter, Late for Church Levite, Pity Me Priest, Serving Samaritan, Hurting Human, Roving Robber #1, Roving Robber #2*

Roving Robber # 1: Hey, Roving Robber #2, wonder if we can find anyone to rob and beat up today on the road to Jericho?

Roving Robber #2: Look *(pointing down the road)*, Roving Robber #1, here comes a man traveling alone. He will be an easy target!

As Hurting Human arrives, Robber #1 and Robber #2 approach him.

Robber #1: What is your name, traveler?

Hurting Human: My name is Hurting Human.

Robber #2: Well, your name fits you well, especially after we get through robbing you!

Robber #1 and Robber #2 pretend to rob Hurting Human and pretend to beat him up. Hurting Human falls on the ground and moans in pain. Robber #1 and Robber #2 exit the stage.

Joe Cool Reporter enters.

Joe Cool Reporter: Hello loyal fans and viewers. I am Joe Cool Reporter, reporting all of the news worth reporting. I'm here on the side of the road between Jerusalem and Jericho with a Breaking News report. Another man has been robbed on this lonely road. Here he is, lying in pain without anyone to help him. He muttered to me that his name is Hurting Human. I'd help him, but who else would report this breaking news, but me! Here comes a religious-looking guy. Maybe he will help.

Late for Church Levite enters and walks on the opposite side from Hurting Human.

Joe Cool Reporter to Late for Church Levite: Sir, do you see this hurting man? Please state your name and tell our audience how you might help.

Late for Church Levite: I'm Late for Church Levite. You want me to help this man? You must be kidding! I don't have time to help this man. I am late for church as it is. I have to preach today.

Joe Cool Reporter: I hope Hurting Human gets help soon. Oh, here comes another guy. This is a busy road today.

Pity Me Priest enters and walks on the opposite side from Hurting Human.

Joe Cool Reporter: You look like a decent man. Please tell our viewers your name and how you might help this man named Hurting Human.

Pity Me Priest: My name is Pity Me Priest. Really, do you think I would stop and help someone bleeding on the side of the road? He is unclean according to Jewish law. If I stop and help, I will be unclean myself. Pity me if that should ever happen!

Joe Cool Reporter: But this man is dying! Will no one help him? I'd help, but I have to report the news as it happens. After all, I am Joe Cool Reporter, and my fans depend on me. I don't mean to brag, but they hang onto my every word! Look, here's come another man. I hope he's willing to help.

Serving Samaritan enters.

Joe Cool Reporter to Serving Samaritan: Sir, over here. What is your name and would you be willing to help this injured and dying man?

Serving Samaritan: My name is Serving Samaritan.

Joe Cool Reporter: Why did I even bother to ask? This man is a Samaritan. The Jews and Samaritans are enemies. He'll never help!

Serving Samaritan: Of course I'll help. This man is my neighbor. He's in need. I'll bandage his wounds and then take him on my donkey to the nearest hospital. They'll take good care of him.

Joe Cool Reporter: But, Serving Samaritan, this man has no money. He can't afford hospital costs.

Serving Samaritan: Don't worry. I'll pay his hospital bills. That's what neighbors are for!

Joe Cool Reporter: In all my years of reporting breaking news, this is a first! I've never seen a Samaritan help a Jew! Serving Samaritan even called this injured man his neighbor! *(Shakes his head in wonder.)* Loyal fans, this is Joe Cool Reporter for Jerusalem Television. I'm live on location on the Jericho Road and reporting good news for a change!

My Family Helps Me Worship

We Gather to Worship, We Leave to Serve

Worship teaches us how to serve God. We serve God when we take what we have learned in worship and apply it to our everyday living. Children are no exception. God has gifted children with many talents that can be used in ministry to others. Through service to others in the church, school, and community, children have opportunities to practice the Christian virtues of hospitality, compassion, and love.

Talk Points for the Week

Ask: What have you heard about serving others when you are in worship?

Talk with your child about times your family has served others.

Make plans to allow your child to serve others in a tangible way.

Family Worship

Set up a worship center in your home. Let the children in the family help you select a place for your worship center and items to place on your worship table.

How to Set Up Your Worship Center

1. Select a small table or card table.

2. Find a cloth to place on your center. Cover the table with the cloth. You might wish to select a cloth that is the color of the liturgical season.

3. Place a picture of your family together. Place a piece of posterboard to be used to plan a family mission project. Place the Bible open to Mark 12:29-31.

Worship God With Scripture

Read Mark 12:29-31.

Read verse 30 from the passage "*You shall love the Lord your God with all your heart, with all your being, with all your mind, and with all your strength.*"

Have family members do the following motions as you read the verse.

- When they say the word heart—have them draw a heart in the air with their fingers.

- When they say the word being—have them wiggle their bodies.

- When they say the word *mind*—have them point to their heads.

- When they say the word *strength*—have them flex their muscles.

Have family members share ways they have loved their neighbors. Remind them that neighbors are not only persons that live in the neighborhood but are any individuals with needs.

Plan a Family Mission Project

Plan together a family mission project. Gather information on organizations in your community that serve others. Select an organization to help. Plan a family tour of the organization, if that is an option. Use the piece of posterboard on your worship table to outline the steps involved in your mission project. Divide up family responsibilities in planning and carrying out your mission project. Try to select a hands-on project, rather than just collecting items.

Ideas: work at a soup kitchen; sort clothes at a clothing store for those in need; invite a lonely neighbor to share Thanksgiving dinner; work with your child's school to help children in need; work together to pick up trash

Pray: God, we as a family want to serve others. Help us as we plan and carry out our family mission project. Jesus, help us to love God and our neighbors. Amen.

13 Children Lead in Worship

Bible Verse: Let the words of my mouth
and the meditations of my heart
be pleasing to you,
LORD, my rock and my redeemer. (Psalm 19:14)

Children will:

- Make plans for a worship service led by the children of your church.
- Be assigned and practice worship parts to share.
- Lead their congregation in worship.

 ## Worship Wisdom

Prior to preaching their sermons, some pastors recite the words of Psalm 19:14 as an opening prayer. In doing so, the pastor reminds the people of his or her own shortcomings in declaring the word of God and seeks guidance from God. The pastor acknowledges his or her own inadequacy but offers him or herself as a humble vessel. The pastor seeks to deliver the word of God with integrity, knowing that it is always a privilege to proclaim God's message to the listener in worship. The pastor desires to offer a vital, relevant message to the congregation, but above all, wants to offer a message that gains the approval of God.

Psalm 19 is often attributed to David, but we are uncertain exactly who wrote the psalm. The psalmist observes the wonder of God's creation. He is awestruck by the wonderful design of a world directed by a loving, caring God. Nature reminds the psalmist that all of creation bursts forth in vibrant colors in praise of Creator God. All of nature flows from the hands of a caring and faithful God. The psalmist views all of creation as a demonstration of God's love and grace. In the eyes of the psalmist, God has created a masterpiece! Furthermore, the psalmist observes God's handiwork in the Torah, the Jewish Law. The Torah, known today as the first five books of our Bible, provides words of instruction, words of discipline, and words of justice. The Torah offers instruction to

the psalmist on how to live his life in ways that are pleasing and acceptable to God.

As the psalmist views God's creation and observes the words of the Torah, the writer hopes that his own words are acceptable and pleasing to God. He also hopes that the thoughts of his heart will honor God. As the children plan their own worship service and then provide leadership for that service, remind them that, like the psalmist, they are seeking to use words, show actions, and lead worship that is pleasing and acceptable to God.

Instruct your children to begin their worship plans by examining their own hearts. Help them think of their leadership in worship as a way to honor God, rather than to center on themselves. Lead them in a quiet time of reflection and prayer before they begin the worship planning process. Remind them that their leadership in worship provides them an opportunity to teach their congregation about the ways children can use their gifts in humble service. However, God does not expect perfection. Even the most trained and experienced worship leader will make mistakes from time to time. Help the children understand that God does not expect their worship service to be perfect and flawless. Rather, God wants children, like adults, to lead and conduct worship in ways that are pleasing and acceptable to God.

 **Enter With Gladness**

As the Children Arrive:

Supplies: *video of children leading worship, video player, or photographs of children leading in worship*

Preparation:

- Greet each child by name. As each child enters, express gladness that he or she is present.

- Have a video playing for the children to view depicting children leading in worship. If your church has used children in leadership roles for a Children's Sabbath or another worship service, show a video of your own children. If not, you might wish to borrow a video from another church where children have led in their own worship service.

- If you have photographs of your church's children leading in worship, display the photographs for the children to see.

View the Worship Center

Supplies: *Bible; paper; pencil; items to place in worship center such as music notes, acolyte lighter, hand bell, hand-held microphone, picture of the children in your worship session, church bulletin, artist's tools such as markers, crayons, paintbrush, paint, or dancer's shoes*

Preparation:

- *Set up a worship center on a small table. Cover the table with a cloth.*

- *Place some items on the table that represent some of the ways the children will be leading in worship.*

- Show the children the items on your worship center.

- Have the children show you ways they would like to serve in the worship service.

- Write down the leadership roles the children mention or ways they tell you they would like to serve. Keep this list before you as you make assignments. Make note of children that you know have good speaking voices, are good at drama, are currently serving as acolytes, who sing in the choir, or who possess other creative gifts. Consider using older children as speakers, elementary children as ushers/greeters, and younger children to pass out bulletins.

- Consult your children's choir director and children's hand bell director and encourage him or her to prepare musical pieces that the children can share in worship.

- Meet with your pastor and worship leaders to secure a date for the children to provide leadership in worship.

 Bible Praise Notes

Learn the Bible Verse

Supplies: *Bibles*

- Hand out Bibles to the children. Show them how to find the Book of Psalms in their Bibles by opening their Bibles in the middle.

- Let them find Psalm 19. Have them place their fingers on the fourteenth verse of Psalm 19. Say Psalm 19:14 together.

Reinforce the Bible Verse

Supplies: *small rocks or stones, one for each child; red markers*

Say: The writer of Psalm 19:14 wanted to please God with both his mouth and his heart. He believed the words that came from his mouth were important, but so were the thoughts in his heart.

- Give each child a small rock or stone to hold in his or her hand.

Say: The psalmist called God a rock. The psalmist believed that God was strong like a rock.

- Have the children say Psalm 19:14 with you as they hold their rocks or stones in their hands.

Ask: How can you please God with your mouth? (say kind words, say "thank you," sing songs of praise to God)

- Have each child draw a red heart on his or her rock as a reminder of the importance of the thoughts in his or her heart.

- Have the children write their names or initials on the other side of the rock.

- Instruct the children to say the Bible verse as they hold up their rocks with the heart on them facing outward.

- Then, instruct the children to say the Bible verse as they hold their rocks close to their hearts.

Say: The psalmist called God a redeemer. The psalmist believed that God helped him at all times.

- Let each child walk up to the worship center and place his or her rock on the worship table. As each child places his or her rock on the worship table, say to each child: "God is your redeemer."

- Let the children take their rocks homes.

 # Let's Learn to Worship

Draw Worship Bulletins

Supplies: 8½- by-11 inch white paper, markers

- Give each child one sheet of white paper. Let him or her draw a cover for your church bulletin for the Sunday in which the children will lead the worship service.

- If you have a theme selected for that day, ask the children to draw their artwork around that theme.

- You can use as many of the children's drawings as you wish for the bulletin cover by duplicating each drawing as many times as needed.

Worship Altars

Supplies: altar cloths; card tables; large containers; a variety of items that would be appropriate for your church altar such as a Bible, candles, children's toys, flower arrangements, crosses, symbols that represent the ways children worship and serve in your congregation, symbols that represent the theme selected for the Sunday your children will lead in worship, or items that represent various liturgical seasons in your church

Preparation:

- Set up a card table for each group of children.

- Place a variety of items that would be appropriate for your church altar table in several large containers.

- Divide the children into groups of about six children. Assign each group a card table to place their items on.

- Let each group select items from the containers to place on their table.

- After the children have arranged their items on the tables, let the children walk around and observe the tables.

- Remind the children that these worship altars are ways to worship God.

- Let each group share about why they selected certain items to place on their table.

- Talk with the children about items they wish to place on the altar table for the worship service in which the children will provide leadership. Select children who wish to work with adults in arranging the altar for this service.

Make Posters

Supplies: *posterboard, crayons or markers*

- Give each child a piece of posterboard. Have the child draw a poster telling the congregation about the upcoming worship service.

- Place the children's posters in strategic spots throughout your church building.

Make Worship Stoles

Supplies: Reproducibles 24-25—pp. 119-120, *strips of white fabric in the shape of a stole and hemmed around the edges, markers*

Preparation:

- *Photocopy the "Symbols" (Reproducibles 24-25).*

- *Recruit a seamstress in your congregation to hem the strips of fabric around the edges.*

- Give each child a piece of white fabric. Let him or her decorate the worship stole with Christian symbols. Have each child write his or her name on the stole.

- Encourage the children to wear their stoles during the worship service in which they will provide leadership.

Worship Invitations

Supplies: Reproducible 23—p. 118, *markers or crayons*

Preparation:

- *Photocopy "Worship Invitation" (Reproducible 23) for each child.*

- Let each child use crayons or markers to decorate several copies of the "Worship Invitation."

- Make plans for the children to distribute the invitation to Sunday school classes or to hand out after a worship service.

 # We Worship God

Practice for the Worship Service

- If you have already assigned parts, use this as a practice time.

- If your service is not planned, use the time to let children read passages of Scripture, call to worship liturgies, litanies, and/or skits. This will help you discover children who have good speaking voices or children that enjoy drama.

- You can also use this time to teach the children how to usher or ways to greet worshipers.

- Make plans for upcoming rehearsal times so that the children can practice in the sanctuary.

- Let parents know what part their child has been assigned.

Sing Hymns of Praise

- Sing some of the hymns the children have learned during the worship sessions.

Prayer Time

Supplies: Leaders' Guide—p. 91

Preparation:

- *Photocopy "My Family Helps Me Worship" (p. 91) for each child.*

- Have the children form a circle and join hands as the closing prayer is said.

- When they hear the word Amen, ask them to continue to hold hands, but raise their hands in the air in praise of God.

Pray: God, we are excited to be able to use our gifts to lead our congregation in worship. Bless each child as we plan together. May the words of our mouths and the thoughts in our hearts be pleasing to you, God, our rock and redeemer. Amen.

- Send "My Family Helps Me Worship" home with each child.

 # My Family Helps Me Worship

Children Lead in Worship

Your child was taught the Scripture verse found in Psalm 19:14: "*Let the words of my mouth / and the meditations of my heart / be pleasing to you, LORD, my rock and my redeemer.*" This verse reminded your child that he or she should use words and think thoughts that are pleasing to God.

The children are going to be worship leaders in an upcoming worship service. Your child has brought home an invitation giving information about this special event. We hope your family will join us.

One of your child's teachers will be in touch with you about what role your child will be asked to share in the worship service. If your child has been given a speaking part, we ask you to practice with your child at home. Whatever part in the worship service your child has been given, help him or her realize that all parts are important in worship. Affirm his or her role.

Talk Points for the Week

Ask your child to share with you about the worship service in which the children will take leadership roles.

Talk with your child about the part he or she has been assigned for the worship service.

Family Worship

Set up a worship center in your home. Let the children in the family help you select a place for your worship center and items to place on your worship table.

How to Set Up Your Worship Center

1. Select a small table or card table.

2. Find a cloth to place on your center. Cover the table with the cloth. You might wish to select a cloth that is the color of the liturgical season.

3. Place some of your family's favorite worship items on the table.

Worship God With Scripture

Cut out a large picture of a mouth and a large picture of a heart. Provide cross stickers.

Read together Psalm 19:14.

Have family members think of words that would please God. When family members name a word, let them place cross stickers on the mouth.

Walk and Worship

Take a family walk. Walk around your neighborhood, at a park, or on a nature trail.

Have each family member look for a small rock or pebble. Remind the family members that the psalmist referred to God as a rock.

As each person picks up a small rock, have the family members say Psalm 19:14 together.

Sit in silence for a few moments as you view the beautiful world and God's handiwork in nature. After a few moments of quiet, have family members share about times in which they served in leadership roles in worship. Affirm the role your child has been given in the worship service where the children will provide leadership. Offer a prayer for your child.

Prayer in the Garden

Return to your home. Gather in your garden or under a tree in your yard. Share a prayer. Thank God by naming items that begin with the letters in the words "FAMILY." Here is a sample prayer:

F – Thank you, God, for friends.

A – Thank you, God, for apples.

M – Thank you, God, for mothers.

I - Thank you, God, for ice cream.

L – Thank you, God, for love.

Y – Thank you, God, for yellow roses.

 # Planning the Worship Service

Involve Every Child

- Be sure that each child has a part in the service. Use older elementary children to speak and read Scripture, use middle elementary children to usher and greet, use preschool children to pass out bulletins (with an adult or older child).

Themes

- Make your service as child friendly as possible. Make use of items that are familiar to children.

- Select a theme for the day and plan the liturgy, hymns, Scripture readings, message, skits, and drama around that theme.

- Use your church bulletin as a guideline or create your own unique worship service.

- Recruit creative adult, youth, or children writers to write prayers, and litanies. If you use resources already written, select ones that remind persons that we are all children of God.

- Let the children write their own creed to share with the congregation.

Sermons

- The sermon time can be a message by older children, a skit, a puppet show, or a children's musical.

- If children are speaking during the sermon time, have them write out their message and practice saying it several times. Give suggestions to the children on topics or Bible passages.

Processionals

- Have the children process into the sanctuary with balloons. Tie the balloons in bunches at the front of the sanctuary.

- Have the children process into the sanctuary waving streamers attached to dowel rods.

- Have the children process in with banners or signs related to your theme.

Music

- Select hymns that are familiar to the children.

- Work with the children's choir director and/or children's hand bell director to involve those groups.

- Invite a child to sing a solo or play a musical instrument

- Teach some of your children a liturgical dance or sign language and have them share the movements.

Prayers

- Allow children to offer prayers, but ask them to write out their prayers.

Art

- Let children draw the bulletin cover, decorate the altar, and create a worship banner or parament for the Communion table.

Offering

- Have children take up the offering in baskets or chicken buckets that they have decorated on the outside, rather than using heavy offering plates for the offering.

- Take up a special offering to go to a worthy cause in your community that meets the needs of children.

Communion

- Allow children to serve Communion to the congregation. Ask your pastor to train the children who will serve. An alternative to Communion is the Wesley Love Feast found in *The United Methodist Book of Worship*. Use stations for the Love Feast. Let the children serve the congregation. Serve fish crackers rather than bread.

Rehearsal

- Always schedule a rehearsal time with the children.
- Let them practice speaking on microphones in the sanctuary. Some churches find it helpful to

take a Sunday school session for practice time since children are already present at church.

- Recruit a good sound technician to work the sound system. Make sure he or she can be present at the rehearsal.

 # Sample Worship Services

Theme: We Are All God's Children

- As worshipers entered the sanctuary, they were given a baggie with crayons to draw a picture of God or the way God works in our world and our lives. These pictures were displayed around the church after the service.

ALL ARE WELCOME (Time of Greeting)

BEGINNING MUSIC (Children's Choir sings)

OPENING SCRIPTURE: Matthew 18:1-5

CALL TO WORSHIP

Leader: No matter how old or young, what gender or color we are,

People: **We are all just children.**

Leader: No matter where we live, or who we live with, what we do, or where we do it,

People: **We are all just children.**

Leader: For we are all God's children, no matter what.

People: **We are all God's children.**

WORSHIP SONG   Halle, Halle, Hallelujah
The Faith We Sing, 2026

(Different age groups of children wrote the verses.)

Verses: Let the little children come to me
The faith of a mustard seed is all you need
We are all God's children, you and me
I am the Lord and God, the only one

CREED (Children rewrote the Apostles' Creed)

SONG OF PRAISE (Children's Choir)

SCRIPTURE READING: Colossians 3:12-17

CHILDREN'S SKIT

HYMN: *Jesus Loves Me*

GOSPEL READING: Matthew 25:35-40

SHARING OUR FAITH (Children shared the sermon time.)

PRAYER TIME

Lord's Prayer – paraphrased by children

Our God, who is holy and lives in heaven, honored by your name.
When God's kingdom comes, the world we live in will be like it is in heaven.
Give us bread because we are hungry.
Please forgive our wrongs, and we will forgive others who sin against us.
Keep us from doing bad things and keep us away from Satan.
God, you are everything. Amen.

OFFERING

DOXOLOGY (Children's hand bell choir plays)

WESLEY'S LOVE FEAST (*Water and fish crackers were served by the children. See* The United Methodist Book of Worship *for Wesley's Love Feast*)

BENEDICTION

Theme: Hospitality

The children renamed parts of the traditional worship service to make the language more child-friendly.

ASSEMBLING OF THE CHURCH—Visitors and members are invited to sign the attendance pads.

ALL ARE WELCOME (Greeting)—Worshipers are welcomed to the service.

WORDS OF WORSHIP (Call to Worship)

Leader: Welcome to God's home.
  In God's home, everyone is welcome.

**People: The young in age and the young in
    heart,
    boys and girls, women and men,
    teenagers and grandparents.**

Leader: Everyone is a part of God's family.

People: So welcome to God's home.

WORSHIP SONG (Hymn)

MORNING PRAYER

Thank you, God,

> that you love us all as your children.

Thank you, God

> that you show us how to love each other.

Thank you, God,

> that you help us love even the people we don't know or don't like.

Thank you, God,

> that you have give us this church to be a home where we can love and be loved.

Thank you, God,

> that you are here with us now and always, welcoming us inside to love and sending us outside to love.

WORSHIP SONG (Hymn)

GOD GIVES THE WORD TO US

> Bible Message: I John 3:1-7

> Hymn (Response to Bible reading)

> Gospel Reading: Luke 24:36b-48

SHARING OUR FAITH (Several children share for the sermon time)

WE ANSWER GOD (Time to Reflect and Respond; Quiet music is played)

CALL TO PRAYER

> Psalm 4 (responsive reading)

> Prayer and Lord's Prayer

(After a child reads each request, the congregation is asked to pray in silence.)

We thank you God for your blessings of food and water, shelter and safe homes . . .

For family and friends . . .

and our church where we worship God . . .

Thank you for our schools where we can learn . . .

(Lord's Prayer)

TIME OF GIVING AND TITHING (Offering)

> Gift to God Song (Doxology)

SONG OF CELEBRATION (Closing Hymn)

GO AND JOIN CHRIST (Benediction)

Theme: World Communion

PRELUDE This Is the Day (Piano solo by child)

WELCOME AND ANNOUNCEMENTS

CALL TO WORSHIP (Children's Choir)

HYMN: *Let Us Break Bread Together*
(The United Methodist Hymnal, 618)

CLEANSING PRAYER (A prayer that calls persons to repentance and offers the forgiveness of Christ.)

THEME FOR THE DAY (Children share about the theme of Holy Communion)

PRAYER (written by a child)

EXPRESSION OF FAITH A Special Meal
(Children share about why Communion is a special time in the church.)

THE LORD'S PRAYER

SPECIAL MUSIC (solo by one of the children)

OFFERTORY PRAYER

On this World Communion Sunday, give us eyes to recognize your reflection in the eyes of Christians everywhere. Give us a mind to accept and celebrate our differences. Give us a heart big enough to love your children everywhere. We thank you for setting a table with space enough for all!

OFFERTORY MUSIC (Children's Hand Bell Choir)

DOXOLOGY

BIBLE STORY: Luke 22:19-20

BIBLE STORY MEMORY VERSE: Luke 22:19b
(Children teach the congregation this verse.)

TEACHING MOMENT

We remember that Jesus was the baby born at Christmas.

We remember Jesus.

We remember that Jesus loved the little children.

We remember Jesus.

We remember that Jesus is God's son.

We remember Jesus.

We remember that Jesus taught us that God loves each one of us.

We remember Jesus.

We remember that Jesus shared a special meal with his friends.

We remember Jesus.

We remember that at the special meal, Jesus held up a cup. He thanked God for things to drink. Then Jesus passed the cup to each of his friends.

We remember Jesus.

We remember Jesus whenever we drink juice and eat bread together at a special meal called Communion.

We remember Jesus.

We remember that Jesus said, "Do this in memory of me."

We remember Jesus.

> From *Touch the Water Taste the Bread: Ages 3-5*, Cokesbury 1998

SPECIAL MUSIC (Instrumental music by child)

PRESENTATION OF THE ELEMENTS (Children carry altar cloth decorated by the children and carry in Communion elements and place them on the Communion table.)

PRAYER OF GREAT THANKSGIVING FOR WORLD COMMUNION SUNDAY (Pastor)

COMMUNION (Children serve Communion.)

SENDING FORTH AS MINISTERS OF GRACE (Benediction)

Bible People Worshiped God

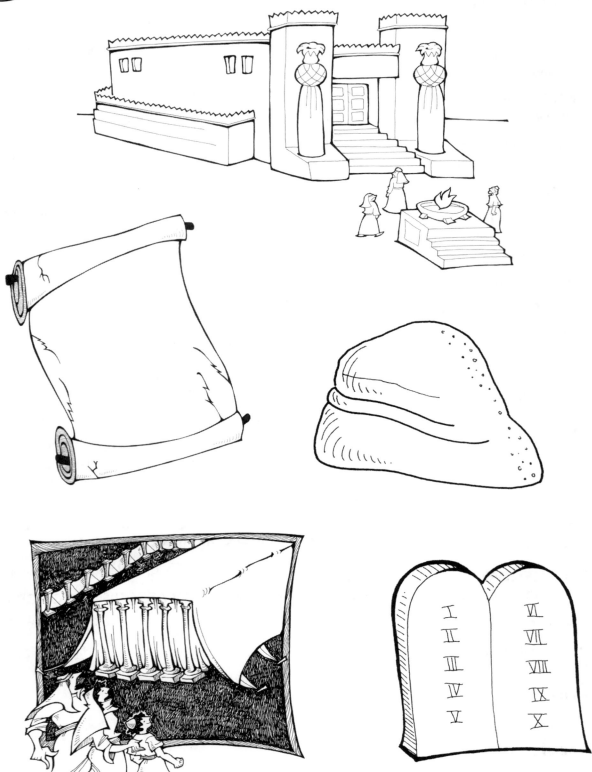

Worship Today

Circle the things that are found in your church.

Worship the Lord With Gladness: God's Children in Worship

Jesus Is Baptized

Connect the dots.

Worship the Lord With Gladness: God's Children in Worship

Shell and Shark Game

Reproducible 5

Remember Jesus

Cut out the puzzle pieces. Mix the pieces. Put the puzzle together.

Worship the Lord With Gladness: God's Children in Worship

Chalice and Bread Patterns

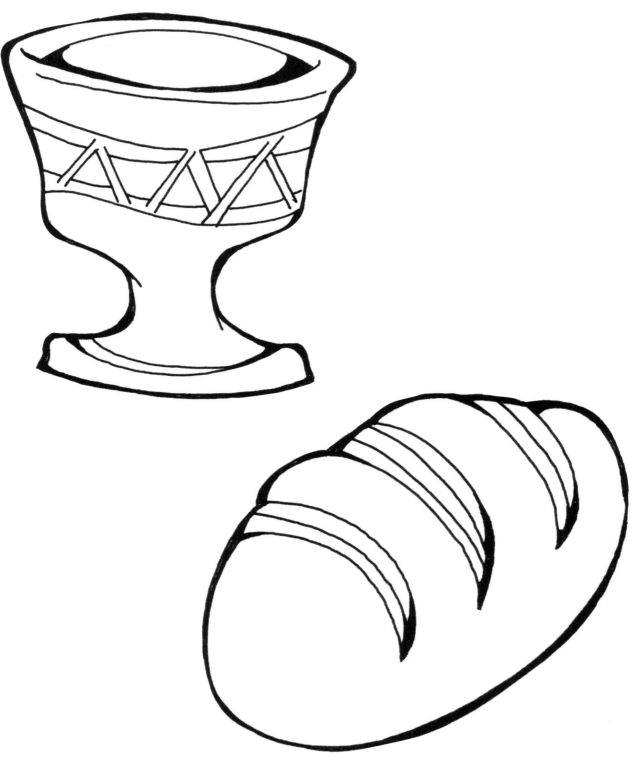

Worship the Lord With Gladness: God's Children in Worship

Worship Leaders

Match the leader to the thing he or she uses during worship.

Worship the Lord With Gladness: God's Children in Worship

Worship Symbols

Draw a line from the explanation to the matching symbol.

God's love through the death of Jesus

Our country, the United States of America

The Christian Church

Jesus as the Light of the World

Creation and life; God's beautiful world

Our gifts to God

Holy Communion

The United Methodist Church

Praise God With . . .

Fill in the blank to discover musical instruments of the Bible.

☆ = E   ♫ = P   ♡ = R   ✿ = S   ☺ = C

ly ___ ___
   ♡   ☆

___ ___ ___ d   ___ i ___ ___
 ♡   ☆   ☆   ♫   ♫   ☆

___ ymbal ___
 ☺   ✿

___ ho ___ ha ___
 ✿   ♫   ♡

lut ___
    ☆

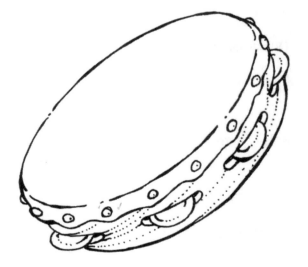

Reproducible 10

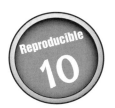

Musical Instrument Search

Find the words in the puzzle below.

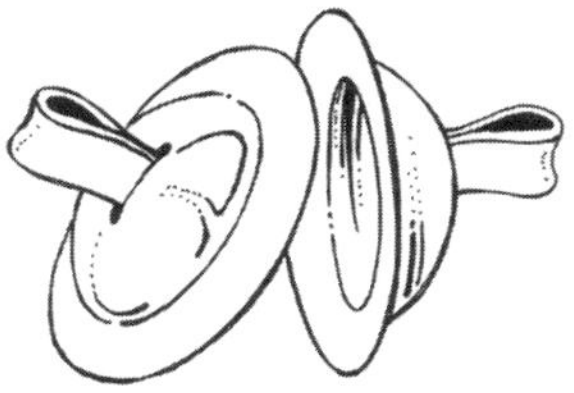

N	V	N	E	L	E	Q	H	V	H
N	G	A	R	Z	Q	P	U	K	X
O	U	Y	Z	O	C	A	I	L	C
M	Z	B	L	K	H	E	W	P	D
U	C	Y	M	B	A	L	S	Q	S
R	S	G	N	I	R	T	S	A	L
D	S	T	E	J	L	C	R	M	T
O	N	H	T	Z	E	C	N	A	D
V	Y	R	U	V	T	E	R	Y	L
L	M	P	L	E	N	C	U	R	W

horn
lute
lyre
drum
dance
strings
pipe
cymbals

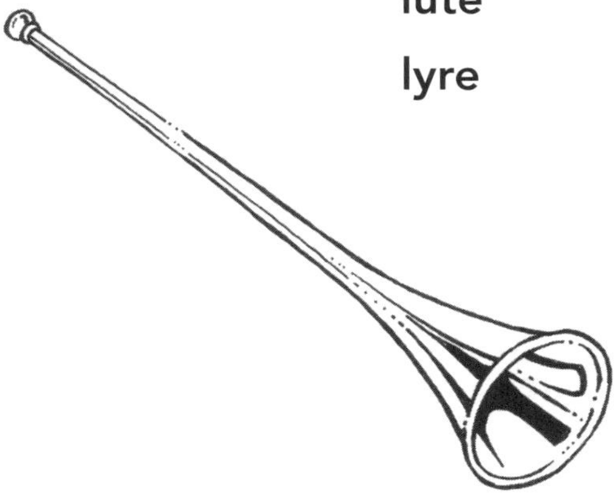

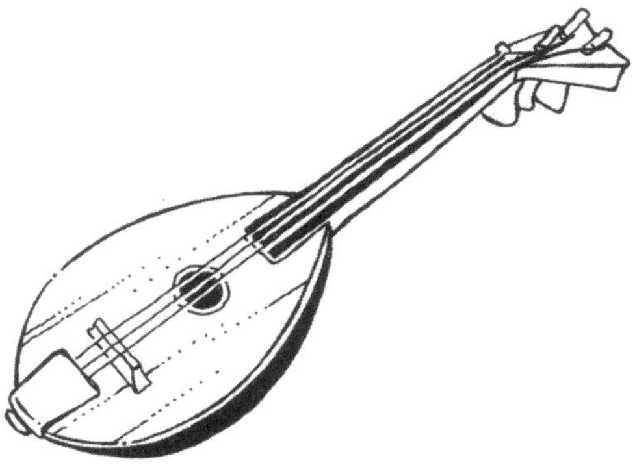

Worship the Lord With Gladness: God's Children in Worship

105

For where | two or three | are gathered | in my | name, | I'm there | with them. | Matthew 18:20

Worship the Lord With Gladness: God's Children in Worship

Worship Words

Draw a line from each word to the matching picture.

| Hymn | Peace of Christ | Benediction |

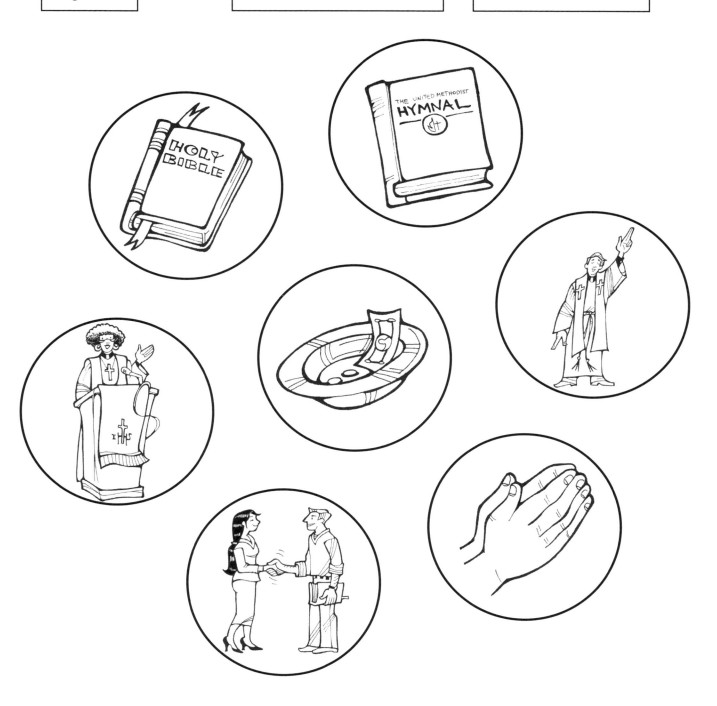

| Sermon | Prayer | Scripture | Offering |

Worship the Lord With Gladness: God's Children in Worship

Apostles' Creed

I believe in God the Father Almighty, maker of heaven and earth;

And in Jesus Christ his only Son our Lord:

who was conceived by the Holy Spirit, born of the Virgin Mary, suffered under Pontius Pilate, was crucified, dead, and buried.

the third day he rose from the dead;

he ascended into heaven, and sitteth at the right hand of God the Father Almighty; from thence he shall come to judge the quick and the dead.

I believe in the Holy Spirit, the holy catholic church, the communion of saints, the forgiveness of sins, the resurrection of the body, and the life everlasting. Amen.

The Apostles' Creed, Traditional Version

The Lord's Prayer

Our Father, who art in heaven
  hallowed be thy name.
Thy kingdom come, thy will be done
  on earth as it is in heaven.
Give us this day our daily bread.
And forgive us our trespasses,
  as we forgive those who trespass
  against us.
And lead us not into temptation,
  but deliver us from evil.
For thine is the kingdom, and the
  power, and the glory, forever.

Amen.

From the Ritual of the Former Methodist Church

Worship the Lord With Gladness: God's Children in Worship

Psalm 95:6

Come, let's worship and bow down!
Let's kneel before the LORD, our maker! (*Psalm 95:6*)

come

worship

and bow down

Worship Word Search

Find the words in the puzzle below.

```
K  M  S  C  M  K  P  S
V  E  X  W  O  N  R  L
R  Z  E  T  S  E  A  O
C  B  S  U  C  E  N  W
P  L  A  N  P  L  C  O
B  U  A  N  Z  N  E  B
S  D  H  P  B  P  K  M
S  L  S  H  O  U  T  F
```

clap   bow   shout
kneel   dance

Worship the Lord With Gladness: God's Children in Worship

Visitor Welcome Cards

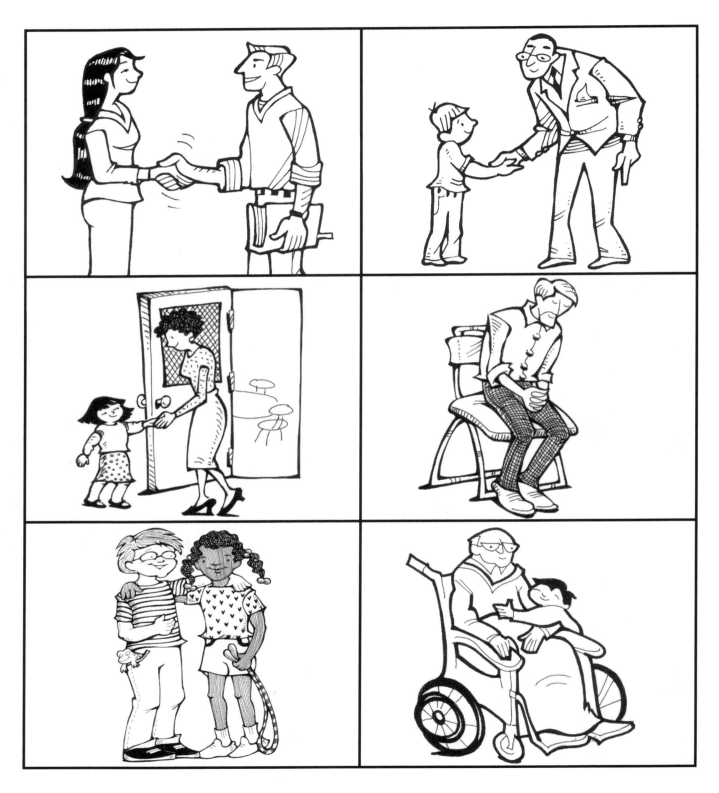

Worship the Lord With Gladness: God's Children in Worship

Hello, Friend!

Please sit with me

at worship on

_____
(date)

at

_____
(time)

See you then!

Worship the Lord With Gladness: God's Children in Worship

Serving God

Stoles for the Church Year

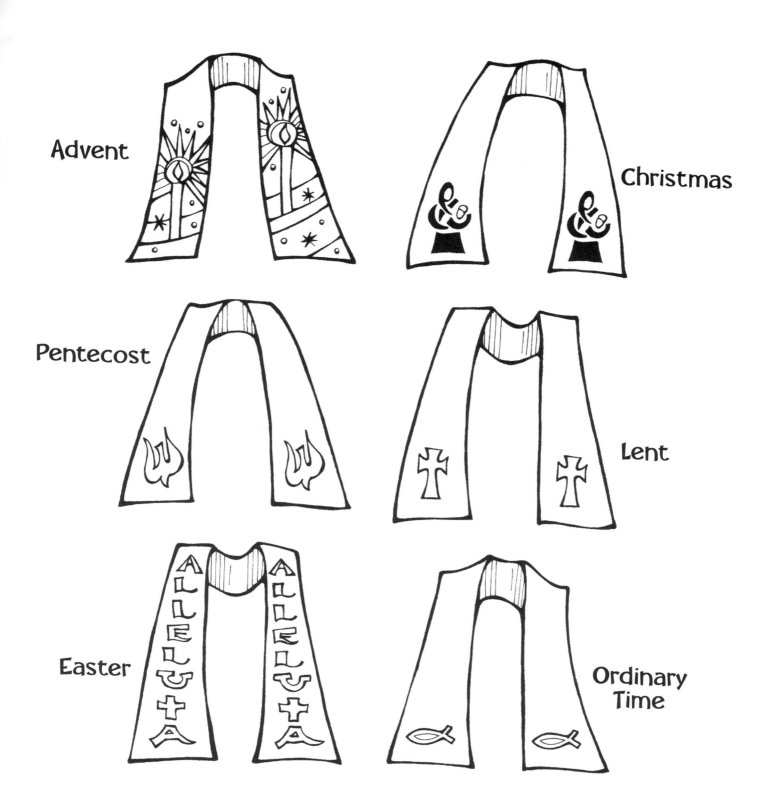

Advent

Christmas

Pentecost

Lent

Easter

Ordinary Time

Worship the Lord With Gladness: God's Children in Worship

Church Year Clock

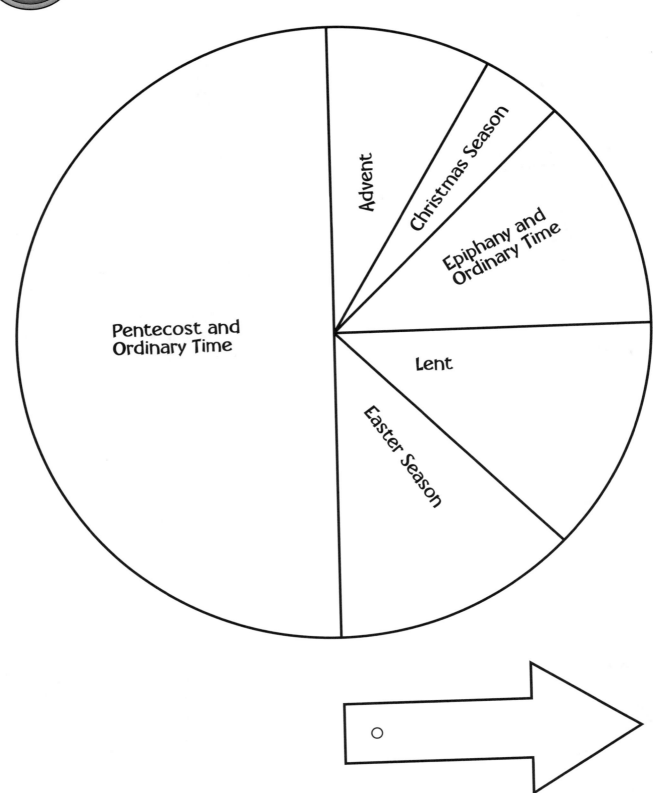

Advent

Christmas Season

Epiphany and Ordinary Time

Lent

Easter Season

Pentecost and Ordinary Time

Unscramble the Verse

Unscramble the letters to find the Bible verse. Look up Mark 12:31 to check your answer.

ovel __ __ __ __

royu __ __ __ __

ehorbing __ __ __ __ __ __ __ __

sa __

reflsuyo __ __ __ __ __ __ __ __

_____

Israel, listen! Our God is the LORD!
Only the LORD! Love the LORD your
God with all your heart, all your
being, and all your strength.

(Deuteronomy 6:4)

Worship Invitation

Come!
Worship the Lord With Gladness!

The children of

_____

(name of church)

will be leading worship on

_____

(date)

at

_____

(time)

Worship the Lord With Gladness: God's Children in Worship

Symbols

Worship the Lord With Gladness: God's Children in Worship

Symbols

Worship the Lord With Gladness: God's Children in Worship